Inspector Calls

by J. B. Priestley

David James

Series Editors:
Sue Bennett and Dave Stockwin

HODDER
EDUCATION
AN HACHETTE UK COMPANY

The Publishers would like to thank the following for permission to reproduce copyright material.

Photo credits

p.10 Topfoto; **p.21** Donald Cooper/Photostage; **p.30** Donald Cooper/Photostage; **p.31** Photostage; **p.36** Bettina Strenske/Alamy; **p.45** Archive Pics/Alamy **p.53** Donald Cooper/Photostage

Acknowledgements

p.11 United Artists on behalf of the Estate of J. B. Priestley; **p.12** *The Independent*.

Every effort has been made to trace all copyright holders, but if any have been inadvertently overlooked, the Publishers will be pleased to make the necessary arrangements at the first opportunity.

Although every effort has been made to ensure that website addresses are correct at time of going to press, Hodder Education cannot be held responsible for the content of any website mentioned in this book. It is sometimes possible to find a relocated web page by typing in the address of the home page for a website in the URL window of your browser.

Hachette UK's policy is to use papers that are natural, renewable and recyclable products and made from wood grown in sustainable forests. The logging and manufacturing processes are expected to conform to the environmental regulations of the country of origin.

Orders: please contact Bookpoint Ltd, 130 Park Drive, Milton Park, Abingdon, Oxon OX14 4SE. Telephone: (44) 01235 827720. Fax: (44) 01235 400454. Email education@bookpoint.co.uk Lines are open from 9 a.m. to 5 p.m., Monday to Saturday, with a 24-hour message answering service. You can also order through our website: www.hoddereducation.co.uk

ISBN: 978 1 4718 5353 1

© David James 2016

First published in 2016 by

Hodder Education,

An Hachette UK Company

Carmelite House

50 Victoria Embankment

London EC4Y 0DZ

www.hoddereducation.co.uk

Impression number   5   4   3   2   1

Year   2020 2019 2018 2017 2016

Cover photo © Photodisc/Thinkstock/Getty Images

Typeset in 11/13pt Bliss Light by Integra Software Services Pvt. Ltd., Pondicherry, India

Printed in Italy

A catalogue record for this title is available from the British Library.

Contents

Getting the most from this guide

This guide is designed to help you raise your achievement in your examination response to *An Inspector Calls*. It is written so that you can use it throughout your GCSE English Literature course: it will help you when you are studying the play for the first time and also during your revision.

The following features have been used throughout this guide to help you focus your understanding of the play.

Target your thinking

A list of **introductory questions** labelled by Assessment Objective is provided at the beginning of each chapter to give you a breakdown of the material covered. They target your thinking in order to help you work more efficiently by focusing on the key messages.

Build critical skills

These boxes offer an opportunity to consider some **more challenging questions**. They are designed to encourage deeper thinking, analysis and exploratory thought. Building and practising your critical skills in this way will give you a real advantage in the examination.

GRADE *FOCUS*

It is possible to know a play well and yet still underachieve in the examination if you are unsure what the examiners are looking for. The **GRADE FOCUS** boxes give a clear explanation of how you may be assessed, with an emphasis on the criteria for gaining a Grade 5 and a Grade 8.

REVIEW YOUR LEARNING

At the end of each chapter you will find this section to **test your knowledge**: a series of short, specific questions to ensure you have understood and absorbed the key messages of the section. Answers to the 'Review your learning' questions are provided in the final section of the guide (p. 101).

GRADE *BOOSTER*

Read and remember these pieces of helpful **grade-boosting advice**. They provide top tips from experienced teachers and examiners who can advise you on what to do, as well as what *not* to do, in order to maximise your chances of success in the examination.

Key quotation

Key quotations are highlighted for you, so that if you wish you may use them as **supporting evidence** in your examination answers. Further quotations, grouped by characterisation, themes and key moments, can be found in the 'Top ten' section on page 93 of the guide.

All page references in this guide refer to the 1992 Heinemann edition of *An Inspector Calls* (ISBN 978-0-435232-82-5).

The Inspector: 'We don't live alone. We are members of one body…' (p. 56).

Introduction

Studying the text

You may find it useful to read sections of this guide when you need them, rather than reading it from start to finish. For example, the section on 'Context' can be read before you read the play itself, since it offers an explanation of relevant historical, cultural and literary background to the text. It is here that you will find information on aspects of Priestley's life that influenced his writing, on the particular issues with which Priestley was concerned and on where the play stands in terms of the literary tradition to which it belongs.

As you work through the play, you may find it helpful to read the relevant 'Plot and structure' sections before or after reading a particular act or section of text. As well as a summary of events there is also commentary, so that you are aware of key events and features in each act of the play. Later, the sections on 'Characterisation', 'Themes' and 'Language, style and analysis' will help develop your thinking further, in preparation for written responses on particular aspects of the text.

Many students also enjoy the experience of being able to bring something extra to their classroom lessons in order to be 'a step ahead of the game.' Alternatively, you may have missed a classroom session or feel that you need a clearer explanation, and the guide can help you with this too.

An initial reading of the section on 'Assessment Objectives and skills' will enable you to make really effective notes in preparation for assessments, because you will have a clear understanding of what the examiners are looking for. The Assessment Objectives are what exam boards base their mark schemes on. In this section they are broken down and clearly explained.

Revising the text

Whether you study the play in a block of time close to the exam or much earlier in your GCSE English Literature course, you will need to revise thoroughly if you are to achieve the very best grade that you can.

You should first remind yourself of what happens in the play, and for this the section on 'Plot and structure' might be revisited in the first instance. You might then look at the 'Assessment Objectives and skills' section to ensure that you understand what the examiners are, in general, looking for.

'Tackling the exams' then gives you useful information on the exams and on question format, depending on which exam board specification you are following, as well as advice on the examination format, and practical considerations such as the time available for the question and the Assessment Objectives that apply to it.

Advice is also supplied on how to approach the question, writing a quick plan, and 'working' with the text. Focused advice on how you might improve your grade follows, and you need to read this section carefully.

You will find examples of exam-style responses in the 'Sample essays' section, with examiner comments in the margins so that you can see clearly how to move towards a Grade 5, and how then to move from a Grade 5 to a Grade 8. When looking at the sample answers, bear in mind that the way responses are assessed is similar (but not identical) across the boards. It is sensible to look online at the sample questions and materials from the particular board that you are taking, and to try planning answers to as many questions as possible. You might also have fun inventing and answering additional questions, since you can be sure that the ones in the sample materials will not be the ones you see when you open the exam paper!

This guide should help you to clarify your thinking about the play, but it is not a substitute for your thoughtful reading and discussion of *An Inspector Calls*. The guide should also help you consolidate your approach to writing well under the pressure of the examination. The suggestions in the guide can help you to develop habits of planning and writing answers that take the worry out of *how* you write, and so enable you to concentrate on *what* you write.

Remember: the examiners are not looking for set responses. You should not read this guide in order to memorise chunks of it, ready to regurgitate in the exam. Identical answers are dull. Instead, use the guide as a springboard to develop your own ideas. The examiners hope to reward you for perceptive thought, individual appreciation and varying interpretations. Try to show that you have engaged with the themes and ideas in the play and that you have explored Priestley's methods with an awareness of the context in which he wrote. Above all, don't be afraid to make it clear that you have enjoyed the play.

The play in performance

Finally, remember that *An Inspector Calls* was written to be seen, rather than read on the page only. You might be fortunate enough to see it as it was originally intended: on stage. But there are also some screen adaptations available: the 2015 BBC production, starring David Thewlis as the Inspector, is well worth watching, even though it does make considerable changes to Priestley's original text. The 1954 adaptation, with Alastair Sim as the Inspector, now appears very dated, but is nonetheless worth watching as it is provides an additional context for your studies. You may also find other versions of the play online, and although each one adapts Priestley's original, all preserve the essential message of the play: namely, that we have a moral duty to care for each other.

As you watch these versions of the play, and as you read and re-read *An Inspector Calls* (and this guide), do not forget that although the play was written to inform and to challenge the audience's views, it was also intended to entertain. Regardless of whether you sympathise with Priestley's views, few can doubt that it does just that, and this perhaps explains its ongoing popularity, in schools as well as with filmmakers and theatre directors. Do remember, however, that your examination is on the play, rather than on a film or television adaptation.

Enjoy referring to the guide and good luck with your examinations.

Context

Target your thinking

- What is meant by 'context'? (**AO3**)
- How did Priestley's life and times influence his work? (**AO3**)
- How did sociological and political conditions in England at the beginning of the twentieth century affect Priestley's view of society? (**AO3**)
- How did other literary forms influence Priestley? (**AO3**)

What is meant by 'context'?

In order to fully understand and appreciate the play *An Inspector Calls*, it is necessary to have some understanding of context. The term 'context' refers to all the circumstances under which a text was produced. It includes the social, political and historical events of the time (such as the end of World War II) and the beliefs that the writer holds about those events, as well as the events leading up to that time. It also encompasses the writer's own personal circumstances, and how his experiences shaped his views. Context can also refer to the artistic influences that contribute to the play's style and structure, in this case the literary context.

An Inspector Calls was written in 1945, the final year of World War II. It is set in 1912, two years before the start of World War I. Priestly was 18 in 1912; by 1945, he had had the opportunity to reflect on his experiences as a young man and to formulate his political beliefs. Keeping these key dates in your mind as you read the text will give you a fuller sense of Priestley's main ideas, as well as helping you to understand how the play works as a piece of drama: its characters, its extensive use of dramatic irony, its setting, its historical references. All these aspects and more are dependent on knowing the play's context. Important though they are, however, it is vital that you see this is a *literary* text written by Priestley, and you should write about how its context shapes it as a work of literature, rather than seeing it purely as a historical document.

Knowing the context of the play and being able to
mention it in your exam response is important, but it
must always be related directly to the question you
are answering. Attaching a 'stand-alone' paragraph on
context at the start or end of your essay won't gain
you many marks. Demonstrating a secure understanding
of Priestley's political views, however, which inform
the moral message of the play, is essential to writing
convincingly about context.

J.B. Priestley

▲ J.B. Priestley

John Boynton Priestley was born in 1894 in Bradford, a Northern industrial town much like Brumley in the play. He therefore lived through 1912 – the time the play is set – and would have had some knowledge of families like the Birlings. He had a reasonably contented childhood although his mother died when he was very young.

Despite having a good education he decided against going to university, preferring instead to begin his working life as a junior clerk (with the stated purpose of gaining life experience), before pursuing his ultimate aim of becoming a writer. Perhaps his experience as a lowly office worker helped him to gain some understanding of the problems faced by the millions of underpaid, ordinary working people of Edwardian England.

At the same time, this was an exciting period of his life, when he enjoyed the company of many of his father's socialist friends. Their frequent, lively political discussions may well have influenced the development of the values he expresses within *An Inspector Calls*.

The young Priestley would also have been familiar with the works of radical or visionary writers such as H.G. Wells and George Bernard Shaw, dismissed as 'cranks' by the 'hard-headed' business man, Arthur Birling.

When war was declared in 1914, Priestley volunteered to join the infantry. At the age of 20 he was sent to the front, and his experiences there were, inevitably, hugely influential in shaping his future views of war. He narrowly escaped being killed on a number of occasions; he saw many of his friends die or suffer terrible injuries, and was himself injured. He therefore understood very clearly the lessons of 'fire and blood and anguish' (p. 56) that the Inspector refers to in the final speech of the play. Many years after the war, he wrote:

'This was no ordinary generation…we believe to this day that the best companions of our youth, the liveliest minds and bravest hearts, all the golden lads…went to that war and never came back from it. This is something that nobody born after about 1904 can ever fully appreciate.'

(J.B. Priestley, *Literature and Western Man*, 1960)

The war no doubt influenced him to choose to go to university to study Modern History and Political Science at Cambridge University, but he realised during this time that he would prefer to be a writer than an academic. From Cambridge he moved to London, where he started in earnest to write essays and book reviews throughout the 1920s. His first novel, *The Good Companions*, was published in 1929 and its success allowed him the freedom to dedicate himself full-time to writing.

From novels he moved into drama. His output was prolific, and through the 1930s Priestley became an increasingly popular – and assured – playwright. He did not limit himself to one particular genre, and wrote domestic tragedies as well as comedies. He was fascinated by the concept of time, believing it to be much more complex than is commonly supposed. In one play – *Dangerous Corner* (1932) – a group of couples endure an evening of crushing revelations before the play returns to its starting point in order for different outcomes to develop. Such a device, as well as themes such as collective responsibility, figure strongly in *An Inspector Calls*.

With the outbreak of World War II Priestley's focus as a writer changed, and he moved on to broadcast journalism with the BBC. His *Postscripts* programmes made him almost a household name. His willingness to criticise the British government's actions, however, as well as his frequent calls for social change, led the series to be cancelled. By now, though, his reputation was firmly established, and his authorial voice clear and self-confident: it was at this time that he wrote *An Inspector Calls*. The play was immediately hugely popular, and was performed around the world (premiering in Moscow). It remains his most famous work.

He continued to write through to the 1970s and died in 1984, aged 89.

Priestley was a remarkably prolific writer, and he influenced public opinion over a long and turbulent period in this country's history. As a novelist, playwright, journalist and broadcaster, his ideas reached a wide and varied audience. Although his voice is distinctively English he was never parochial, and he became immensely popular around the world with readers who sympathised with his views on social justice. His legacy survives: much of his work remains in print, and his political views continue to inspire successive generations.

Build critical skills

Priestley was a supporter of the Suffragettes' cause, and even wrote an introduction to Antonia Raeburn's *The Militant Suffragettes* in 1973. Some critics would argue that *An Inspector Calls*, with its focus on the struggle between the classes, is essentially socialist; others might claim because of its concentration on the exploitation of a young woman that it is an early feminist drama. Which do you think is correct? Can both interpretations be valid?

Build critical skills

The play's characters, setting and focus on the class divisions affecting the country in 1912 are recognisably English, and yet it remains very popular in many different countries. Why do you think this is?

Performance history

An Inspector Calls remains Priestley's most enduring work for a number of reasons. It is a 'well made play', tightly written, with a very clear focus on the plot and themes. It is also a cleverly, economically constructed piece of drama that is immediately accessible to most audiences. Importantly, the characters and the audience move from a position of ignorance to one of knowledge and understanding of themselves and the world around them.

The play was first performed in Moscow in 1945 and then performed in London in 1946. It quickly moved to Broadway in New York where it ran for a number of months. The play has been revived on a number of occasions, and has remained popular in repertory theatres ever since it was first performed. It was with the National Theatre's 1992 revival, directed by Stephen Daldry, however, that the play gained a new lease of life: this was a radically re-imagined production, with a striking set design that incorporated non-naturalistic staging to convey important conceptual ideas about the divisions in society.

Daldry's production was seen as an attack on the politics of the British Conservative Party of the time, and in particular those that had been introduced by the former Prime Minister Margaret Thatcher (who once famously claimed that 'there is no such thing as society'). It could perhaps be argued that *An Inspector Calls* is revived on screen or on stage in times of political unrest and that as such it reflects the issues thought to be relevant to society at the time. The recent 2015 BBC production, for example, was screened just after the Labour Party had been defeated in the general election, and some commentators saw parallels between some of the themes Priestley was exploring and both the growing number of dispossessed refugees from Africa and the Middle East seeking refuge in Europe and the huge numbers of families in the UK living below the poverty line and dependent on food banks.

> **GRADE BOOSTER**
>
> The director Stephen Daldry has said that his production was 'a call to arms for collective responsibility against the wild, unregulated, and purely profit-driven selfishness that's created vast levels of unemployment and distress throughout the world' (*The Independent*, 25 September 2009). A comment on how you see the relevance of the play today can demonstrate to the examiners that you have thought deeply about your personal response.

Set as it is in 1912, and being first performed in 1945, it is a play that seems rooted in war. But in fact both dates, ominous though they might be for us, could also be associated with hope: Mr Birling's speech in which he references the *Titanic*, although dramatically ironic, works because it would have been believable at the time: 1912 was a time of relative prosperity, and great advances in engineering and science. World War I, however, was a cataclysmic event, which for a while obliterated any sense of optimism. Priestley was appalled both by the war and by the treatment of veterans afterwards. Perhaps the greatest irony is that all of the problems referred to by Mr Birling as being over and done with are still with us today.

▲ World War I soldiers in their trench

Although Europe had been left in ruins by 1945, it was still a time of hope for many: after all, Nazism had been defeated, and the Allies had defeated the greatest threat to freedom in mankind's history. It seemed an apt moment to attempt to ensure that the mistakes of the past were not repeated, and to build a better future for everyone. In setting the play in 1912, it has been suggested that:

'Perhaps, ever preoccupied with time…he wanted to rewind history to the point when things could have turned out differently.'
(Dr John Baxendale, in a programme article for a production of the play at the Canadian Shaw festival, 2008)

Key quotation

'Look at the progress we're making. In a year or two we'll have aeroplanes that will be able to go anywhere. And look at the way the automobile's making headway – bigger and faster all the time.'
(p.7)

The social and political context

The play explores conflict in a very wide sense: the arguments that simmer below the surface in the Birlings' family home before the Inspector's arrival, and which erupt under his interrogation, are domesticated versions of larger themes that can be seen in the great issues that shaped the world during this time. For some (such as the war poets Siegfried Sassoon and Wilfred Owen), it was the older generations who had sowed the seeds of war, and the younger generations who suffered. The dispute that sees Eva Smith sacked by Mr Birling is a small event symbolising the class conflict that saw much social unrest at the beginning of the twentieth century (the British Labour Party was founded in 1906, six years before the play is set).

The deep trends that were shaping society at the time are evident throughout *An Inspector Calls*. Sheila develops from being a girl who is 'rather pleased with herself' into a self-confident young woman who is unafraid of expressing her opinions. This personal growth, which sees her able openly to question her parents, reflects the growing political pressure from, among others, the Suffragettes, to secure the vote for all women. It would be 1928, however, before the vote ('suffrage') was extended to all women over the age of 21.

Capital versus labour

Like his father, Priestley was a **socialist**. This means that he supported a political and economic system that was based on both collective responsibility and collective ownership of important industries and other sectors of society. These views are often referred to as being 'left wing', but be cautious when using that term as it can refer to a huge range of political views.

The huge conflicts between **free-market capitalism** and more state-controlled socialist systems dominated the twentieth century, ensuring that old certainties began to crumble. The rigid class systems in Europe were beginning to crack as rapid industrialisation saw an increasingly large and affluent middle class develop. World War I was undoubtedly responsible for disrupting the old class system as working-class men, for perhaps the first time, fought side by side with public school officers. But such change was already happening in 1912, as we can see in Mr Birling: he is a 'self-made man', the personification of how someone born into relatively modest means could rise through the social ranks, marrying someone his 'social superior' and, as the play starts, be on the verge of an honour from the King. His children are securely middle class and it is a further sign of their upward mobility that Sheila is getting engaged to Gerald Croft, the son of wealthy, titled parents, at the start of the play.

> **Build critical skills**
>
> To what extent are Eva Smith and Sheila Birling mirror-images of each other, both personifying very different experiences of what it meant to be young and female in England in 1912?

> **Socialism:** has many different forms, but those who subscribe to a form of state control of major industries, with the government taking ownership of major companies, would be described as socialists.

> **Free-market capitalism:** an economic theory that allows companies to compete with each other with a very limited role from the state.

Such changes, however, are put into context by Priestley throughout the play because they clearly benefit only those who are already powerful and affluent, and those who (like Birling) are prepared to be ruthless in their treatment of their employees. For many, like Eva Smith, opportunities to improve one's prospects were few and far between: her journey from rural poverty to insecure work in a factory, to shop assistant and then to prostitution, shows a representative range of jobs available to young, working-class women at the time. Life was hard and uncertain for many such women. There was no benefit system. Those without the means to support themselves had to depend on charity, and charity was dispensed by the wealthy, such as Mrs Birling, and so was not always dispensed adequately or fairly.

In order to protect their rights, and to secure better pay, many workers joined a trade union. Trade unions were organisations that would campaign to try to ensure that their members were not exploited by bosses such as Mr Birling. Although trade unions had been legalised in this country in 1871, they often had very little power. When relations between bosses and workers broke down, the unions would sometimes go on 'strike', which is what happened at the Birling factory, with Eva as one of the organisers. For Birling it is his 'duty' to 'keep labour costs down'. Eva loses her job not just for striking, but for acting on behalf of others. She shows a sense of duty to her fellow workers, and is punished by Birling for doing so. Priestley's sympathies are very clearly with the workers and, symbolically, it is through the younger generation that we see a growing unease at the uncaring approach to other people promoted by Birling's form of capitalism (it is Eric who states, simply, that his father 'could have kept her on instead of throwing her out', p.15).

The outbreak of World War I disrupted many of the social issues that Priestley is exploring, but they did not go away. Indeed, when 'normal life' resumed in 1918, social unrest – the 'Capital versus Labour agitations' – intensified. The country had not only lost a huge number of men in the four years of conflict but, as a result of the war, rationing had been introduced on food, coal and petrol. By 1921 there were more than 2 million unemployed in the UK.

The wider political context

The problems that this country was encountering were, if anything, worse in Europe. The defeated Germany, weighed down with huge 'reparation' costs (effectively having to pay the victorious Allies for the cost of the war), saw a deepening depression spread through its economy. The new Nazi Party, led by Adolf Hitler, promised the people an end to the ongoing hardships and humiliation they felt had been heaped on them by the Allies. By 1933 Hitler had been elected Chancellor of Germany and six

Build critical skills

It could be argued that Mr Birling's opening speeches represent him as too obviously wrong about too many important subjects and that, as such, his credibility as a rounded character never recovers. To what extent would you agree with this view?

years later saw the outbreak of World War II. Russia's class system, which like Great Britain's had as its head of state a ruling monarch, underwent equally profound change: the Bolshevik Revolution in 1917 saw a Communist government, led by Vladimir Lenin, sweep away the old order. But the hope that saw this happen faded with Lenin's death, as Joseph Stalin – a leader responsible for as many deaths as Hitler – established a brutal dictatorship, which would last for many years.

And yet in 1912 there *was* real optimism about the future, if not among those at the bottom of the social hierarchy, then certainly for the new middle class. Great Britain was a powerful force on the world's stage, and the country took particular pride in its naval forces: Britain, in the words of the popular song, seemed to 'rule the waves' and this was perhaps symbolised in the building of the 'unsinkable' *Titanic*. For Birling this 'unsinkable' ship represents 'facts' and 'progress' (p. 7).

But the *Titanic* was not unsinkable, and when it hit an iceberg in the North Atlantic on its maiden voyage it dealt a blow not just to shipping, but also to the self-belief of the country. Of course, that Birling has these views is another example of dramatic irony: his unshakeable faith in the *Titanic* is at odds with the eventual reality. The audience must ask itself: if we cannot trust him on this, what else will he get wrong? How good is his judgement? In many ways the *Titanic* becomes one of the most evocative symbols in the whole play, and one that predicts much of what is to come, both within the text and beyond: the hopes and dreams of the Birlings are about to sink, proving that nothing is certain and nobody is immune to the sometimes harsh realities of life. But the sinking vessel also captures both the hope and despair of a period about to be marked by terrible loss: within two years Europe would be involved in a war that would teach everyone, regardless of class, harsh lessons in 'fire and blood and anguish'.

Literary context

In writing *An Inspector Calls*, Priestley was influenced by a number of different theatrical forms.

Greek drama

Classical Greek drama conformed to the unities. The three unities consist of:

- Action: the plot has one storyline.
- Time: stage time and real time are the same.
- Place: only one setting is used.

An Inspector Calls conforms to all three unities, and because of this it remains a tense, tightly organised drama. With all three unities working together successfully (in other words, the setting is appropriate to the action, and the time maintains the appropriate essential pace) there is little to distract the audience from focusing on the author's main themes. Another element that the play borrows from Greek drama is the chorus – conventionally this was a group of actors who commented on the play's actions but did not intervene. Clearly, the Inspector is the **choric** device in this play, although he is clearly not just a commentator but is also a key character who directs much of the action.

Common to both Greek and Shakespearean drama is a sense that the major characters – and by extension the audience – move from a position of ignorance to one of knowledge, and in doing so experience a moment of **catharsis**, which cleanses them of the difficulties they are experiencing: this process can be a source of comedy, or tragedy, but it has to show that something has been learned.

Choric: commenting on events and characters in the style of a dramatic chorus.

Catharsis: a process of release and relief in a drama or in life.

Morality plays

The morality plays of the medieval period were hugely popular **allegories**, exploring the Seven Deadly Sins (pride, sloth, gluttony, envy, covetousness, lust and anger). Each play sought to reject the vices displayed, and to turn the main protagonist towards a life dedicated to God. We could try to match each of these sins to characters in the play, but the broader message – that a good life involves behaving selflessly – is a perennial truth not confined to any genre or period.

Allegory: a story, or a poem, that has a strong moral (or political) message.

Other genres

An Inspector Calls is often referred to as 'a well-made play': its parts work together to create a powerful tale of morality. It is effective – and memorable – because it keeps the audience interested throughout. The well-made play, often very conservative in form and subject matter, dominated popular theatre in Europe in the nineteenth and early twentieth centuries. Common features of such plays include:

- A significant part of the plot that has already happened before the play begins.
- An opening scene in which characters and their contexts are introduced.
- Letters, or other missives, that find their way to the wrong people, often revealing a secret.
- Acts that end with moments of climax.
- A happy ending that resolves the key issues.

Priestley was clearly influenced by this form, and he appropriates some elements (such as much of the plot in *An Inspector Calls* having taken place before the curtain goes up), but he also subverts it. For instance, the subject matter is not the comfortable, bourgeois concerns that often characterise these plays, but something more radical; the ending, too, is not a happy one.

Priestley also borrows from, but redefines, another hugely popular genre: the 'whodunnit'. Detective stories, and murder mysteries, had been hugely popular in fiction from the nineteenth century (with Arthur Conan Doyle's Sherlock Holmes books and stories being the most famous example). The detective is often an unconventional outsider figure, who is gifted with an ability to see things and solve mysteries that others cannot. Priestley's Inspector fits this description but, again, the play does not present us with a simple mystery, nor does it have a body or a murderer. Not only is the crime is not solved by the end but we do not even know if there has been a crime!

And so the 1940s audience would have been challenged on a number of different levels. The subject matter itself would have been provocative but, as we can see, the various conventions from different theatrical traditions would have been both familiar and disconcertingly unfamiliar at the same time, rather like the Inspector himself.

REVIEW YOUR LEARNING

(Answers are given on p. 101.)

1 What is meant by the term 'context'?
2 Where was Priestley born?
3 What were his experiences of World War I?
4 What did Priestley do during World War II?
5 When is the play set, and why is this significant?
6 When and where was the play first performed?
7 Who were the Suffragettes?
8 What are the three unities?
9 Can you define (and distinguish between) capitalism and socialism?
10 What could the *Titanic* be seen to symbolise?

Plot and structure

Target your thinking

- What are the main events of the play? (**AO1**)
- How do these events unfold, act by act? (**AO1**, **AO2**)
- How does Priestley use structure to develop the plot? (**AO2**)

Main events

Act One

- The Birlings are celebrating the engagement of Sheila to Gerald Croft.
- Mr Birling gives speeches about the 'steadily increasing prosperity' of the country and tells Gerald that he is expecting a knighthood.
- The Inspector arrives and tells them that a young woman has committed suicide. Her name is Eva Smith.
- Birling admits that he knows Eva Smith and that he sacked her for leading a strike.
- It is revealed that Eva had been hired at Milwards but had been sacked after a customer – who turns out to be Sheila – complained.
- We learn that Eva changed her name to Daisy Renton and that Gerald had an affair with her.

Synopsis of Act One

The play opens with a scene of great comfort and luxury – featuring cigars, port and the remains of a fine dinner. Priestley states in the stage directions that the light should be 'pink and intimate' (p. 1), perhaps suggesting the rosy glow of complacency. The Birlings (Mr and Mrs Birling, their son Eric and their daughter Sheila) are celebrating the engagement of Sheila to Gerald Croft at their large home in Brumley, 'an industrial town in the North Midlands' (p. 1). Mrs Birling's superior social status is established when she reprimands her husband for a lapse in etiquette when he praises the dinner. Priestley hints that all is perhaps not well between Sheila and Gerald through her mention of his absence the previous summer.

Mr Birling holds forth about the 'steadily increasing prosperity' of the country, and about the great progress being made in many areas (for instance, in engineering). He states categorically that there is no chance

Key quotation

Mr Birling: '...I gather there's a very good chance of a knighthood – so long as we behave ourselves, don't get into the police court or start a scandal – eh?' (laughs complacently)
(p. 8)

Build critical skills

What do you think Priestley was hoping to achieve dramatically by introducing the Inspector at this precise point in the play? What would be the effect on the audience of this sudden loud noise?

Build critical skills

Why do you think Priestley shows the contrasting reactions of father and son? What might he be beginning to suggest to us?

Key quotation

Sheila: 'But these girls aren't cheap labour – they're people'
(p. 19)

of war, and that the *Titanic* is unsinkable. This clearly will have an impact on an audience, who know that the *Titanic* did in fact sink and that two years later there was a terrible war.

Left alone with Gerald, Mr Birling seems to indicate that his happiness over the engagement is more to do with the potential benefits to his business. He tells Gerald that he is expecting a knighthood. A joke is made about the need to avoid trouble over the next few months; a clear sign to most audiences that the opposite will in fact occur! At this point Eric, who has been drinking steadily over the course of the evening, returns to the room. Priestley very skilfully offers us more clues as to what will come – Eric's drinking will prove over the course of the play to have created problems for him.

Mr Birling continues to speak about how he sees the world: he tells both men that a man has to 'mind his own business and look after himself' (p. 9). Before he can finish this speech, however, he is interrupted by 'a sharp ring of a front door bell' (p. 10) and the Inspector is introduced. This is clearly a dramatic moment, perhaps a symbol of a wake-up call or the intrusion of the outside world.

Inspector Goole tells them that a young woman, Eva Smith, has committed suicide by taking strong disinfectant. She has left behind a letter and a diary. The Inspector tells Mr Birling that he'd once employed this young woman in his factory and shows him (but not the other characters) a photograph of her. Mr Birling admits that he knows Eva Smith: she had led a group of girls demanding a rise in pay; when Birling refused they went on strike for two weeks before returning defeated, when Birling sacked Eva. He responds to the Inspector impatiently, as if the news is a tiresome inconvenience; Eric, in contrast, is shocked by the news ('My God!', p. 11). Birling attempts to justify his actions in terms of his duty to 'keep labour costs down', a statement that suggests both greed and insensitivity.

There follows a disagreement, in which Gerald supports Birling's actions.

Key quotation

Gerald: 'You couldn't have done anything else.'
(p. 15)

Eric, however, supports the Inspector's criticism of Birling and Gerald, claiming that 'he could have kept her on instead of throwing her out' (p. 15), thus establishing a clear difference between the two young men. At this point Sheila returns to the room and the Inspector tells her of the suicide. Like Eric she is shocked and upset by the news.

Inspector Goole then goes on to tell the next stage of Eva's story: after losing her job she became increasingly desperate, before getting a position as a shop girl at Milwards, but she was then dismissed after a customer complained about her. Sheila is shown a photograph and reacts with horror.

'He produces the photograph. She looks at it closely, recognises it with a little cry, gives a half-stifled sob, and then runs out.'
(p. 21)

Sheila soon returns and tells the story of how she had made a complaint about Eva, which was what resulted in the loss of her job. Sheila had been keen on a dress that clearly had suited the very pretty Eva much better, and she had become very annoyed when she saw Eva smiling in the mirror when Sheila had tried it on. She therefore demanded that Eva be dismissed. This reflects the enormous power wealthy people had over the poor and how they exploited them. Sheila is filled with regret over what has happened and does at least accept her responsibility for what happened to Eva.

The Inspector reveals that soon after losing this job Eva changed her name to Daisy Renton; this news is met with a strong reaction from Gerald, and his response is noticed by other characters. At this point the Inspector leaves the room with Eric to find Mr Birling, leaving Gerald and Sheila alone. Gerald confesses that he had an affair with Eva (who he'd known as Daisy) and rather shamefully pleads with Sheila not to mention it to the Inspector. Sheila's perceptive intelligence is highlighted when she tells him that the Inspector already knows. The Inspector re-enters the room and looks 'steadily and searchingly' (p. 26) at both characters.

▲ The Inspector (Philip Stone) with Sheila (Jeanette Ranger) in the 1973 Mermaid Theatre production

Act Two

- Mr and Mrs Birling return.
- Gerald reveals the details of his affair with Daisy, which he broke off after a few months. Upset by the news of Daisy's death, he leaves to go for a walk. Sheila breaks off their engagement.
- Mrs Birling initially claims she does not know Eva, but under pressure from the Inspector admits that she refused to help her. The Inspector reveals that Eva went to Mrs Birling's organisation for help because she was pregnant.
- Mrs Birling claims that the blame for the girl's death lies with the baby's father.
- Act Two ends with Eric, the father of the unborn child, returning to the room.

Synopsis of Act Two

Act Two begins immediately after Act One ends, but the tension is rising. Cracks begin to emerge in the relationship between Gerald and Sheila as they start to argue; the Inspector then takes charge, explaining to Gerald that Sheila has to see that she is not solely to blame for Eva's fate: 'if there's nothing else, we'll have to share our guilt' (p. 29).

Mrs Birling returns to the room after being told by Mr Birling why the Inspector has called. Her attitude seems at odds with what has just been seen on stage and Sheila warns her mother to be careful what she says, but Mrs Birling ignores her, condescendingly saying that the Inspector appears to 'have made a great impression' on Sheila (to which the Inspector claims, mysteriously, '…we often do on the young ones', p. 30). Here Priestley is hinting at an idea that later emerges more strongly – that any hope of change lies with the younger generation.

Sheila tells her mother that Eric has been 'steadily drinking too much for the last two years', preparing us for the later revelation of the extent of Eric's irresponsibility. Mrs Birling is shocked, suggesting that she has little knowledge or understanding of her own children. She becomes increasingly defensive. Sheila continues to warn her mother not to 'build up a kind of wall between us and that girl', because the Inspector 'will just break it down' (p. 30).

Mr Birling returns and admits that he has been unable to persuade Eric to go to bed, to which the Inspector says that he will want to question him later on, thus implicating Eric in the plot. Initially, Gerald tries to deny his involvement with Daisy but the Inspector, increasingly supported by Sheila, persists and Gerald tells of how he met Daisy in the Palace Bar, rescuing her from Alderman Joe Meggarty. Mrs Birling is 'staggered' by the mention of the Alderman, though Sheila confirms that everyone knows of his reputation. This might suggest Mrs Birling is unaware of events in her own town or that she is blinded by status.

Gerald explains that Daisy stood out from the usual 'hard-eyed, dough-faced women', being 'very pretty' (p. 34). It is revealed that she was 'desperately hard up' (p. 36) and actually hungry, thus creating more audience sympathy. They became lovers soon after.

Their affair did not last long and Gerald describes how he broke it off, and also how 'gallant' (p. 38) Daisy was in accepting his decision. He goes on to tell the Inspector how Daisy had saved some money, and the Inspector in turn tells him that she went away to a seaside town for two months, 'to be alone, to be quiet, to remember all that happened between you' (p. 39). During that time she kept a diary, which the Inspector has seen. Her quiet dignity in this period increases audience sympathy still further.

Gerald is upset by the realisation that Daisy is dead and asks to go for a walk. Before he goes Sheila hands her engagement ring back to him, claiming that they 'aren't the same people who sat down to dinner here' (p. 40). Sheila notices that Gerald has not been shown a photograph of Daisy; before she can explore this further, however, the Inspector shows a photograph of a girl to Mrs Birling, who claims she does not know her. The Inspector accuses her of not telling the truth. Mr Birling angrily asks for an apology, which the Inspector refuses to give, claiming that he is simply doing his duty.

The front door slams and Mr Birling goes to find out who has left, returning shortly afterwards to say it is Eric. The Inspector tells them it is important that Eric returns; this leaves Mr and Mrs Birling bewildered and further increases tension. Mrs Birling admits that she had met Eva Smith and that she had refused to help her when she came to the Brumley Women's Charity Organisation two weeks before. One of the reasons for refusing her help is that Eva had used the name 'Mrs Birling', which she thought was impertinent. It appears that Mrs Birling's charity work is motivated by ego and self-importance rather than genuine charitable feelings. She is unapologetic, claiming that the young woman 'only had herself to blame' (p. 43) for her fate. Indeed, she claims that she was only doing her duty in turning her down for help.

The Inspector then reveals that Eva went to Mrs Birling's organisation for help because she was pregnant. Sheila calls Mrs Birling's actions 'cruel and vile' (p. 45). Mr Birling begins to worry, not about the poor girl, but about the possible damage to his reputation and his chance of getting the knighthood, thus confirming his utterly callous and selfish nature.

Mrs Birling tells the Inspector that Eva had told her she turned down the offer of financial help from the father of her child because she suspected the money had been stolen, thus showing her moral fortitude.

Key quotation

Gerald: 'I suppose it was inevitable. She was young and pretty and warm-hearted – and intensely grateful. I became at once the most important person in her life.'
(p. 37)

Build critical skills

When Sheila returns the ring to Gerald, Mr Birling says 'Now, Sheila, I'm not defending him. But you must understand that a lot of young men–' (p. 40).

What do you think he was about to say before Sheila stops him? What does this tell us about young men and sexual freedom at that time? Why else might Birling want the engagement to continue?

Build critical skills

How does the Inspector's strategy of showing a photograph to one character at a time add to the tension of the play?

Key quotation

Mrs Birling: 'I blame the young man who was the father of the child she was going to have... He should be made an example of...'
(p. 47)

In a moment of deep irony Mrs Birling insists that the responsibility for the death of Eva lies with the father of her baby, a 'drunken young idler' who 'ought to be dealt with very severely' (p. 48). Sheila continues to warn her mother to stop talking as it is now obvious that the father being talked about is Eric. The tension increases and the Birlings, both 'frightened' (p. 49), suddenly realise the consequences of Mrs Birling's actions. Act Two ends with Eric returning to the room, 'extremely pale and distressed' (p. 49).

Act Three

- Eric explains that he seduced Eva while drunk, with the result that she became pregnant.
- He admits that he stole money from his father's office to support her and to pay for his drinking.
- Eric learns of how his mother refused Eva help and accuses her of having killed both Eva and the child.
- Before Eric leaves, the Inspector reminds them all that their actions have helped kill Eva Smith.
- Gerald returns and reveals that there is no Inspector Goole on the local force.
- For Sheila and Eric the news does not make a difference. Gerald claims that if each photograph they have been shown is of a different girl then they are not all responsible for the death of Eva Smith.
- After ringing the infirmary Gerald confirms that there have been no suicides for months.
- Gerald offers Sheila the engagement ring but she says it is too soon to think about becoming engaged again.
- The telephone rings and Mr Birling answers it. It is the police, who tell him that a girl has committed suicide and that an inspector is on the way to question them. The play ends with them staring at each other 'guiltily'.

Synopsis of Act Three

Act Three begins immediately, in terms of time within the play, after Act Two ends. Eric enters the living room and immediately realises that the other characters know about his involvement with Eva. Before he begins to tell his story, he asks for a drink. Stage directions state that he is clearly at ease with 'quick, heavy drinking' (p. 51), an impression that Priestley has been building from Act One.

Eric tells the Inspector that when Eva became pregnant, she did not attempt to get him to marry her because she was aware that he didn't

Build critical skills

Eric: 'I wasn't in love with her or anything – but I liked her – she was pretty and a good sport–' (p. 52).

To what extent does Eric's treatment of Eva reinforce the idea that young women of a lower social class could be used as playthings by the wealthy and then thrown aside?

love her, again confirming her strength of character. He also admits that he stole money from his father's office to support Eva. This causes Mr Birling to lose his temper with him again.

At this point Sheila and Mrs Birling re-enter and Eric learns that his mother refused Eva help; he accuses her of killing both Eva and her own grandchild in what is perhaps the most emotionally intense moment in the whole play. The Inspector interrupts the Birlings' argument to remind them that the actions of each one of them helped kill Eva Smith; he tells them that although Eva is dead there are 'millions and millions of Eva Smiths and John Smiths still left with us' (p. 56). He warns the Birlings that we have a responsibility to each other, and that if we 'do not learn that lesson, then they will be taught it in fire and blood and anguish' (p. 56).

The Inspector leaves and Mr Birling immediately starts to worry about the scandal that will damage his chances of a knighthood; Sheila thinks there was something odd about Inspector Goole and speculates about whether he really was a policeman. She talks about how he made each of them 'confess' (something that Mr and Mrs Birling deny happening to them). Mr Birling accuses his children of being fooled, or 'bluffed', by the Inspector who was, in his view, 'probably a Socialist or some sort of crank'. The family begin to argue about what this might mean for them individually, before Gerald returns from his walk. He reveals that he met a police sergeant, who told him that there is no Inspector Goole on the local force. Mr Birling confirms this new information by telephoning Colonel Roberts, the Chief Constable. Both Gerald and Mr Birling believe that the whole business is a hoax, and this alarms both Sheila and Eric: they are shocked that their parents and Gerald think the fact that the Inspector is a fraud makes any difference. For them, the facts remain the same, Eric claims that 'the girl's dead and we all helped to kill her – and that's what matters' (p. 65).

Gerald continues to consider the evidence of the evening: he claims that the photographs they each saw could have been of different girls, which means they are not all responsible for the death of the same girl. Again, they seek confirmation and Gerald telephones the infirmary and learns that there have been no suicides for months. For Mr Birling this is 'proof positive' that the whole story is 'moonshine' (p. 70), an elaborate lie. Both he and Gerald are relieved by the news but Sheila and Eric remain uneasy. Although Gerald sides with the Birling parents, suggesting that he shares their values, the other members of the younger generation believe that everything they have admitted to being involved in did happen; Sheila is frightened by her parents' behaviour, claiming that they were beginning to learn something and now it has stopped. Mr Birling tells her that she is being hysterical.

Build critical skills

Some find the final lines of the play an anticlimax; others enjoy the sudden, final moment of suspense. Why do you think Priestley chose to conclude the play with another proposed visit from a police inspector?

Gerald offers Sheila the engagement ring but she says it is too soon to think about becoming engaged again. At this moment the telephone rings 'sharply' in an echo of the first ringing bell in Act One. It is the police, who tell Birling that a girl has committed suicide and that an inspector is on the way to question them. The play ends with the Birlings and Gerald looking 'dumbfounded', with each of them staring at the others 'guiltily' (p. 72).

Timeline of events

The better you know the order of the events in the play and mentioned in the play, the more secure you will be in writing about important elements in the play, such as dramatic irony and foreshadowing.

Date	Event
September 1910	Eva Smith is sacked by Mr Birling for asking for a pay rise and for leading a group of workers out on strike for two weeks.
December 1910	Eva gets a job at Milwards, a good shop in Brumley.
Late January 1911	Eva is sacked by Milwards after Sheila Birling complains about her conduct.
March 1911	Eva (now going by the name Daisy Renton) and Gerald meet at the Palace Bar; he moves her into a friend's flat and they soon become lovers.
Early September 1911	Gerald finishes the affair; Eva leaves Brumley for two months and writes a diary about recent events.
November 1911	Eva and Eric meet and become lovers.
December 1911– January 1912	Eva discovers she is pregnant; Eric is the father.
Late March 1912	Eva goes to the Brumley Women's Charity Organisation for help but is refused by Mrs Birling.
Early April 1912	The Birlings are gathered at their house in Brumley celebrating Sheila's engagement to Gerald Croft. During the after-dinner speeches Inspector Goole calls, investigating Eva's suicide.

Structure

It is not hard to see how tightly structured *An Inspector Calls* is, with key ideas being developed gradually and eventual plot developments being carefully prepared. The ringing of the doorbell in Act One, for instance, is counterpointed by the ringing of the telephone at the end of the play.

The play is divided into three acts, and each act ends on a moment of unresolved suspense: at the end of Act One we are about to find out the nature of Gerald's relationship with Eva; at the end of Act Two we are about to find out about the nature of Eric's relationship with Eva; at the end of Act Three we are left waiting to discover if the whole cycle of the play is repeated, perhaps until every character accepts responsibility. There are no individual scenes in these acts, but they have distinctive episodes, often marked by a central character leaving or entering the action.

Gustav Freytag suggested that plays could be broken down into common phases:

- **Exposition:** This provides a general introduction to the characters, their backgrounds, and the context or atmosphere, and begins to introduce the key themes. In *An Inspector Calls*, this takes place in Act One until the arrival of the Inspector.

- **Rising action:** Complicating factors are introduced, adding to the tension. Birling, Sheila and Mrs Birling learn their part in Eva's death.

- **Climax:** This is the key moment in the play. The moment when Eric confronts his mother with the full impact of her actions and the Inspector gives his final warning to them all.

- **Falling action:** Falling action refers to the part of the plot that develops immediately after the main climax of the play. Doubts are raised about the true identity of the Inspector.

- **Resolution:** Plot lines and characters are accounted for and resolved. It becomes clear that only Sheila and Eric have changed, with the result that the phone rings and they discover that a young woman has committed suicide.

To some extent these all apply to *An Inspector Calls*, although it could be argued that there is no final resolution – such as there is in a classical or Shakespearean tragedy – as the action looks likely to be repeated endlessly, or until something (such as repentance by all the characters) breaks it.

Entrances and exits

Entrances and exits are used by Priestley to drive the action of the play. Information is revealed or withheld from particular characters in order to increase drama at certain points in the play or for practical reasons to do with the plot. For example, the Inspector's first entrance has been carefully managed by Priestley; importantly, he comes into the room when Sheila and Mrs Birling, two of only three female characters we see on stage, have left the room to allow the men to smoke, drink port and talk about important issues (such as Mr Birling possibly getting a knighthood). Edna removes herself as soon as she shows the Inspector in, leaving an entirely male set of characters to discuss Eva Smith's story – reflecting their dominance.

Build critical skills

Look carefully at the entrances and exits whenever they occur in the play, and consider the effect they have on the action.

This changes when Sheila re-enters 'gaily' (p. 2). Sheila's presence at this stage is important for a number of reasons: while she is directly involved in Eva's fate, equally important is that she asks questions and makes judgements that the other characters are either are unable to do or are unwilling to state openly (it is Sheila who says that girls like Eva 'aren't cheap labour – they're *people*', p. 19). In this way, she probably becomes the character with whom the audience most identifies.

Similarly, Gerald and Sheila are left alone on stage when the Inspector exits to find Birling, and so can discuss Gerald's affair with Daisy. It is important that they are alone together so that they can freely discuss something so emotionally painful, and during this discussion their characters are further revealed.

GRADE *FOCUS*

Grade 5

To achieve Grade 5, students will show a clear and detailed understanding of the whole text and of the effects created by its structure.

Grade 8

To achieve Grade 8, students' responses will display a comprehensive understanding of explicit and implicit meanings in the text as a whole and will examine and evaluate the writer's use of structure in detail.

REVIEW YOUR LEARNING

(Answers are given on p. 101.)

1 How many acts is *An Inspector Calls* divided into?
2 In which fictional town is the play set?
3 What are the Birlings celebrating when the play begins?
4 Why did Mr Birling sack Eva Smith?
5 What reason does the Inspector give for showing one photograph to one person at a time?
6 Why does Sheila break off the engagement with Gerald?
7 Where did Gerald meet Eva?
8 What name does Eva use when she appeals to Mrs Birling for some help?
9 Who does Eric accuse of killing Eva?
10 Where is Eva taken after she dies?

Characterisation

Target your thinking

- Who are the key characters in the play? (**AO1**)
- How does Priestley present the characters on stage? (**AO2**)
- What purposes are served by the characters? (**AO1**, **AO2**)

Mr Birling

From the first moments of the play, Priestley uses stage directions to present Arthur Birling as a 'prosperous manufacturer' (p. 1). The use of stage directions is one of Priestley's most important techniques (see p. 52 in the 'Language, style and analysis' section for further discussion of this topic). Birling is 'heavy-looking', 'portentous' and in his mid-fifties, a description that perhaps suggests someone who is set in his ways, unlikely to change and likely to dominate others. Birling's personality is reflected by his home and possessions, as Priestley tells us that in his 'suburban' house the furniture is 'solid', creating an atmosphere that is 'heavily comfortable, but not cosy' (p. 1). The impression created of his home is, like that of Birling himself, one of weight: this is an imposing – and not very welcoming – place.

Priestley also tells us that, influential though he is, Birling is 'provincial in his speech', meaning that although he is socially mobile, with a big house, his accent will always reveal his more modest origins. This theme of class is further developed by Priestley's description of Mrs Birling as being 'her husband's social superior'. As we shall see, class is a source of tension, not only in the society of the time, but right at the heart of this marriage. Negative though his description is, Birling is not simply a caricature of a capitalist who enjoys 'a good cigar': his manners are 'fairly easy' and he is sociable, and this can be seen at the start of the play as he is hosting a party to celebrate the engagement of his daughter – Sheila – to Gerald Croft.

This party is important to Birling because what matters to him is status and money; Gerald's parents have titles, Sir George and Lady Croft, and the proposed marriage may provide an opportunity to work more closely together in the future with Gerald's father's company 'for lower costs and higher prices' (p. 4). It is as if the impending marriage is also a merger between two businesses, enabling the rich to get richer and the poor poorer. We can see the injustice of this, but Birling cannot.

Key quotation

Mr Birling: 'We hard-headed practical business men must say something sometime. And we don't guess – we've had experience – and we know'
(p. 7)

Build critical skills

Re-read Mr Birling's early speeches: do you think Priestley's portrayal of him risks making him a caricature of a businessman, or do you believe that we can respond to him as a rounded – and flawed – character?

▲ Mr Birling (Campbell Singer) in the 1973 Mermaid Theatre production

Dramatic irony: a technique used by writers that allows the audience to know more about an event, or another character, than the characters on stage know.

Key quotation

Mrs Birling: 'When you're married you'll realise that men with important work to do sometimes have to spend nearly all their time and energy on their business. You'll have to get used to that, just as I had.'
(p. 3)

In addition, Priestley seems to suggest that it is this aspect of the marriage rather than his daughter's happiness that appeals to Birling, as he attempts to persuade her to overlook Gerald's infidelity when she breaks off the engagement.

Lack of self-awareness is a defining characteristic of Birling. He is unmoved by the difficulties his workforce face: for him 'community' is 'nonsense' and all those who believe that 'we were all mixed up together like bees in a hive', each depending on each other, are 'cranks' (p. 10).

He makes it known to everyone how important he is, even suggesting that he might be above the law ('I was an alderman for years – and Lord Mayor two years ago – and I'm still on the Bench', p. 11).

In these early speeches Priestley uses **dramatic irony** to reveal how profoundly wrong Birling is about key issues, and in doing so he allows the audience to judge Birling's later actions. If he can be so wrong about the *Titanic* ('absolutely unsinkable'), the imminence of war ('impossible'), Russia (it 'will always be behindhand naturally', p. 7), and the future (the world of 1940 will be one of 'peace and prosperity', p. 7), then he can also be wrong about everything else. By the end of the play he is exposed as a fool who has learnt nothing; what is more worrying, however, is that it is fools like him who, for Priestley, run the country.

Mrs Birling

As well as being Birling's social superior, Mrs Birling is described by Priestley as being 'about fifty' and 'a rather cold woman' (p. 1). She lacks compassion and understanding, not only with those like Edna who serve her, but even for her own children. Priestley suggests she is somewhat removed from the society that has shaped her. She is shocked by revelations about Alderman Meggarty being a sexual predator and that there are 'women of the town' (p. 34) in Brumley, and she views Gerald's affair with Eva as 'disgusting' (p. 38). For her, men and women have clearly defined, and very traditional, roles to fulfil. Instead of basing her judgements on evidence, she chooses instead the narrow prejudices of the social snob.

Build critical skills

The role of women in society is under constant scrutiny in the play, but status complicates matters. Mrs Birling has influence: what point do you think Priestley is making about gender and status in the play? Which do you think determines a character's fate more?

She patronises almost every other character at some point, describing her daughter as 'an hysterical child' (p. 48) and her son as 'only a boy' (p. 32), and in these easy acts of linguistic infantilisation Priestley shows that she is able to avoid reality.

This would not matter except that, throughout the play, we see that her failure to understand, and her selfish attitudes (which become manifest through actions), have serious consequences.

It is Priestley's presentation of her treatment of Eva Smith, however, that is the most illuminating. At her lowest ebb Eva turns to the Brumley Women's Charity Organisation for help, and it is Mrs Birling who turns her down. She rejects Eva because she suspects that she told 'a pack of lies', and because Mrs Birling believes that responsibility rests with the individual, not with society; but she goes further, attempting to dignify her decision as her 'duty' (which contrasts very sharply with the Inspector's sense of moral and public duty).

Perhaps worse than all this is that she is a hypocrite, as Priestley shows us in dramatic fashion. She initially insists that whoever got Eva pregnant 'ought to be dealt with very severely' (p. 48) but, when that man is revealed to be Eric, she avoids accepting responsibility of any kind, claiming that she did not know it was him. When the true horror of her – and her family's – actions are revealed she initially appears frightened, but this soon passes and she, quicker than most, is happy to reassert her former, inviolable position, as long as her public reputation remains intact.

Build critical skills

Mrs Birling seems to not know her own children at all, and she seems distant from her husband. Do you think we are to feel any sympathy for Mrs Birling? Or is she without any redeeming qualities?

Key quotation

Mrs Birling: 'As if a girl of that sort would ever refuse money'
(p. 47)

▲ Judy Parfitt plays Mrs Birling in Stephen Daldry's Aldwych Theatre production (1993)

Certainly Priestley makes it clear that her prejudiced view of the world is reasserted at the end: she is relieved to discover that Inspector Goole is a 'fake', pointing out that 'I couldn't imagine a real police inspector talking like that to us' (p. 62), implying that in Brumley everyone knows their place in the hierarchy, including the forces of law and order. For Mrs Birling the Inspector 'never even looked like one' (p. 63) – a telling remark, and one endorsed by her husband who firmly states that 'it makes *all* the difference' (p. 63). Appearance, for them both, proves to be the only measure that counts.

GRADE **BOOSTER**

Remember that showing an awareness of the different perspectives on characters can bring depth to your analysis. However, you will need to support each point with evidence from the text and also to ensure that your argument is clear and coherent.

Sheila Birling

Appearance also matters to Sheila Birling. The stage directions describe her as 'a pretty girl in her twenties, very pleased with life and rather excited'. It is a succinct but revealing description, as we will see as the play continues. Not only is she attractive, but she is also, like her parents, impressed by outward show. Being pleased with life also suggests that, like her mother, she has been indulged and insulated from anything that threatens her cosy view of society. Lastly, it is her tendency to get excited and to act hastily that results in the dismissal of Eva from her only good job (Eric astutely observes of Sheila that 'she's got a nasty temper sometimes', p. 5).

And yet Priestley uses her to represent hope in the play. Unlike her parents (and Gerald), who represent the old order filled with vested interests, she is, like her brother, part of a 'younger generation' who can make a difference. The Inspector recognises this, admitting that the 'younger ones' are 'more impressionable'. Because she is prepared to change, and learn, she is seen by some as a more complex character than her parents. It is interesting to analyse why she changes: is she motivated by a sense of duty to others? Or is it more personal than that? The answer is probably both: she appears genuinely remorseful about her involvement in Eva Smith's fate, promising that 'I'll never, never do it again to anybody' (p. 24), and she, more than any other character, supports the Inspector in his interrogation of each character. But Priestley shows how she also changes as she learns to become more adult. By the end of the play she is no longer the 'childish', indulged daughter, nor is she the fiancé of Gerald; she chooses instead to assert her own individuality rather than becoming a younger version of her mother. And yet Priestley seems to be hinting that Sheila was never just the frivolous girl she might appear to be. Stage directions reveal her to have 'mock aggressiveness', she is 'half playful, half serious', and 'quiet and serious'.

Key quotation

Shelia: 'If she'd been some miserable plain little creature, I don't suppose I'd have done it.'
(p. 24)

Key quotation

Sheila: 'You and I aren't the same people who sat down to dinner here. We'd have to start all over again, getting to know each other'
(p. 40)

To some extent, Priestley perhaps intended Sheila and Eva to be mirror images of each other, both being young, attractive, principled; but with very different lifestyles. It is true that being female and young, both have limited life choices, but Eva's options are very much worse. Only Sheila has any influence, and she uses that power irresponsibly. While the Inspector recognises her role in Eva's death, he says that although Sheila contributed to her suicide it was her father who started it. Her remorse seems real, though, as she moves from being distressed to quickly trying to tell the truth. But can the audience ever forgive her for her role in Eva's sacking from Milwards? It is one of the most vindictive of all the damaging actions carried out against Eva because it is motivated purely by jealousy.

Key quotation

Sheila: 'Well, he inspected us all right'
(p. 66)

Eric Birling

Priestley describes Eric as being in his 'early twenties, not quite at ease, half shy, half assertive' (p. 2). As the play progresses we learn that he is a heavy drinker, a liar, a thief, and the father of Eva's illegitimate, unborn child. It perhaps says a lot about the other characters that, despite these flaws, he emerges from the play with some credit and, like his sister, is one of the few points of hope.

Also like his sister, Eric has been given a head start in life: he went to a good school, and then on to university, before returning to work for his father (which was not uncommon then). The probing questions he asks of his father go beyond common familial difficulties; indeed, Priestley uses him as a dramatic device, because in answering these questions Birling further reveals how wrong he is. It is Eric who asks if war is a possibility, and it is Eric who points out how unfair his father was in sacking Eva for asking for a pay rise. His voice sometimes seems very close to Priestley's own.

This hostility towards his parents grows as the play progresses, and it is also fuelled by drink. It is Gerald who confirms, in Act Two, that Eric is a hardened drinker, and this is underlined in Act Three when, in an example of **illustrative action**, he reaches for a whisky, 'his whole manner of handling the decanter and then the drink shows his familiarity with quick heavy drinking' (p. 51). Does he drink because of his unhappy relationship with his parents? Or has this relationship been damaged by his drinking? To some extent Priestley leaves this up to us to decide, but the fact that his mother had not noticed his drinking is illuminating, and tells us just how distant they are; and in one of the most revealing comments of the play Eric says that his father is 'not the kind of father a chap would go

Build critical skills

Complex characters develop over the course of a play or a novel, whereas 'flat' characters remain more static, often, like Edna, representing a simple idea. Look at how Priestley develops certain characters – like Sheila – making them more complex through their words and actions, as well as through his stage directions.

Key quotation

Eric: '...and then one of those cranks walked in – the Inspector. (Laughs bitterly) I didn't notice you told him that it's every man for himself.'
(p. 58)

Illustrative action: when character's action illustrates an aspect, or a trait, of their personality.

to when he's in trouble' (p. 54), hence his secretive behaviour. With the exception of Eva, he is the unhappiest character in the play, which might explain why they were attracted to each other.

Priestley seems to suggest that Eva was the responsible adult in this relationship: Eric was 'in a hell of a state' (p. 53) about the pregnancy, but Eva declines his offer of marriage, not only because he does not love her, but because he is immature.

Like his sister, Eric changes over the course of the play: he grows up from being 'a kid' to a young man who takes responsibility for his actions. He also takes responsibility for the failures not only in others but in the system they have helped create; what matters to him is that an innocent young woman is dead and the family are responsible. His awkwardness, his innocence, have been replaced with some hard-earned knowledge, and at the end of the play he seems to know much more than his father.

Gerald Croft

Gerald Croft is introduced by Priestley as 'an attractive chap, about thirty, rather too manly to be a dandy but very much the well-bred young man-about-town' (p. 2). He appears to be everything that Eric is not. He is 'just the kind of son-in-law' Birling always wanted (p. 4). He is the son of Mr Birling's main business rival; importantly, though, the Crofts are more established, their business is bigger, and no doubt they are not only richer but also more comfortable with their status: there is no need to ostentatiously drink port or smoke cigars (Gerald does not, claiming he 'can't really enjoy them', p. 8). Gerald has all the ease and social self-assurance that Arthur and Eric Birling do not have: he is the authentic voice of the Establishment, whereas the Birlings are new arrivals, unsure about how to act in their new social positions.

> **Build critical skills**
>
> Gerald symbolises the Establishment: his family are landed gentry and are affluent. Perhaps more than any other character he emerges from the play with his reputation – if not his engagement – intact. Why do you think Priestley does this?

Priestley aligns Gerald with Birling in terms of their attitude to business. They are as one over the dismissal of Eva Smith ('we'd have done the same thing' he says to the Inspector, p. 17). Gerald suggests that the workers in Birling's factory were probably 'all broke – if I know them' (p. 15) because they were coming back after the holidays. The comment is revealing because it patronises the working class, suggesting that they have acted irresponsibly in their holidays, spending all their money.

Build critical skills

To what extent do you think that Priestley wants us to see Eric as a victim? He might come from an affluent family, but he seems starved of love, isolated and without any real sense of direction in his life. His drinking could be a symptom of his unhappiness. What does this say about money, and class, in this play?

Key quotation

Eric: '...she treated me – as if I were a kid' (p. 53)

Key quotation

Eric: 'It's what happened to the girl and what we all did to her that matters...' (p. 65)

Gerald is implying that if they had behaved more responsibly they would not have been in that position, which is ironic given later revelations about his own irresponsible behaviour.

Like Eric (who offers to do the honourable thing and marry Eva) and Mr and Mrs Birling, Gerald has a conventional view of how men and women should behave. He seems to want to protect Sheila from knowing the details of his relationship with Eva, claiming on her behalf at the start of Act Two that she has had 'a long, exciting and tiring day' (p. 27). Of course, he really wants her out of the way while he is questioned. Priestley suggests that he is mainly motivated by self-preservation. There is also an assumption, however, that such frank discussions, involving sex, are for men, not women.

And it is sex that originally motivates Gerald to behave in the way he does, at least to begin with. He is attracted to Eva (or Daisy Renton as he knew her) but the relationship quickly develops into something more meaningful. He made her 'happier than she'd ever been before' (p. 39). He became 'the most important person in her life' (p. 37) or, in the withering words of Sheila, her 'Fairy Prince' (p. 38). For him it is not a 'disgusting' affair, but something more important and thus Priestley shows us a man who is perhaps weak and egotistical but not wholly bad.

To a certain extent, it might be argued that Gerald's treatment of Eva reflects well on him. He made her happy for a while and left her with a little money. He also appears to be genuinely upset by her fate. On the other hand, it could also be argued that he begins an affair with her when she is at her most vulnerable, knowing he will not marry her, and while he is engaged to the eminently more 'suitable' Sheila. Nor did he trouble himself to find out what happened to her afterwards.

Sheila, who breaks off the engagement soon after hearing the details of the affair, admits that she respects him more than ever before because of his honesty. From this point Gerald's status within the play grows: it is he who takes charge after the Inspector's departure; it is he who retains some objectivity, arguing 'very cleverly' that the Inspector's claims are fabricated; and it is he who telephones the infirmary to find out the fact of Eva's suicide.

And yet Priestley shows that, like the Birlings, Gerald is also very happy to believe that everything has returned to normal, once the Inspector's claims have been questioned. He has apparently learned nothing from the evening, either about himself or about society. His final words articulate, more than anything else, his self-interested complacency:

'Everything's all right now, Sheila. (*Holds up the ring*) What about this ring?'

(p. 71)

Key quotation

Gerald: 'She told me she'd been happier than she'd ever been before' (p. 39)

Build critical skills

Both Gerald and Eric see Eva, initially at least, in sexual terms; Mr Birling values her only as a worker. Do you think that the male characters are represented too negatively in the play or is Priestley's characterisation more complex than it might first appear?

Build critical skills

Does Priestley present Gerald as a man who is truly in love with Sheila? Can you find any evidence in the text to support or to challenge this idea?

Key quotation

The Inspector conveys 'an impression of massiveness, solidity and purposefulness. He is a man in his fifties, dressed in a plain darkish suit. He speaks carefully, weightily, and has a disconcerting habit of looking hard at the person he addresses before actually speaking.'
(p. 11)

Build critical skills

How do you respond to the Inspector as a policeman? Is his tone firm and his style exacting, or is he impatient, judgemental and bullying? To what extent does the tone that this character creates add to the play's power?

Inspector Goole

Priestley makes Inspector Goole intentionally mysterious (even his name conjures up connotations of the ghostly or supernatural, being a pun on 'ghoul'). He is, of course, very different from the other characters in the play: he is an outsider, a man who often refers to his 'duty', which is closer to a moral crusade than the conventional responsibilities of a policeman's job. Priestley creates a charismatic, enigmatic character who dominates the stage and, of course, demands the characters' undivided attention, and their willingness to confess their crimes. For some, this quality, combined with his passionate intolerance of social injustice, makes the Inspector something of a religious figure, like a priest or even a prophet sent from the future to warn those in the past of the terrible mistakes they are making.

His entrance is symbolic: it comes immediately after Mr Birling has dismissed the idea of community as 'nonsense' and is indicated by 'a sharp ring', a discordant noise shattering the comfortable self-congratulations of the Birlings' party. As the rich drink port it is Edna, the sole working class character on stage, who obediently lets the Inspector in. Mr Birling inadvertently predicts how the Inspector will illuminate matters by asking for 'some more light' as he enters.

Priestley's stage directions are always positive about the Inspector, constantly affirming his authority: he has an air of 'solidity and purposefulness' (p. 11). He is 'imperturbable' (p. 31) and speaks with 'calm authority' (p. 55). He takes charge 'masterfully' (p. 55), 'cutting in' (p. 54) to maintain the intensity and momentum of his questioning. He acts as on-stage director, or editor, moving the other characters around the set, making suggestions, bringing others in, stopping them if they speak for too long or threaten to distract us from the plot.

▲ The Inspector (Nicholas Woodeson) in the 2009 production at the Novello Theatre

Priestley gives the Inspector an intensity: he does not so much talk as interrogate. He intimidates other characters, and there is a barely concealed threat to his demeanour, as well as an urgency (he frequently complains that he does not have much time, implying, in fact, that time is running out for all of us); he is blunt, bordering on rude, constantly interrupting characters as they desperately try to justify their actions. His authority is only ever really challenged after he has left. His behaviour is unconventional, and in some respects he is not simply a policeman, but also prosecutor, jury and judge. For some critics he is Priestley's voice on stage: a strong defender of the rights of the working class, and a stern critic of those who refuse to admit their guilt and those who deny the opportunity to repent.

The Inspector plays several roles: he is the storyteller who joins the various narrative strands together into one coherent whole. He tells us important dates, as well as key facts. He does not offer forgiveness because such atonement can only be obtained if the individual is truly repentant. What he can do is create the self-awareness to make this possible. He seems to achieve this with both Eric and Sheila, and in his final speeches, which resemble sermons, he warns us all that unless we recognise how 'intertwined' our lives are and how 'we are responsible for each other' then the cycle of 'fire and blood and anguish' (p. 56) will never be broken.

GRADE BOOSTER

```
Always remember that the characters in the play have
been created by the writer: they are constructs
intended to provoke strong reactions from the audience.
You need to focus on the ways the writer has developed
these characters, and so you have to avoid writing
about them as if they are real people. Use Priestley's
name regularly, or 'the author', 'the writer' or
'playwright': if you simply repeat characters'
names you might be at risk of re-telling the story
and, crucially, losing any real objective, critical
distance.
```

Eva Smith (Daisy Renton)

Like Inspector Goole, Eva Smith dominates *An Inspector Calls*, but she is presented by Priestley as even more of a ghostly presence than he is — never appearing and changing identities depending on who is speaking about her. Although she never appears on stage we know a lot about her from the other characters, which allows us to consider how effective characterisation does not always require the character to be present. She is described by Gerald as 'young and fresh and charming' (p. 35); the Inspector describes her as 'out of the ordinary' (p. 12); Mr Birling calls her 'good looking…a good worker' (p. 14); Sheila remembers her as being 'very pretty…with big dark eyes' (p. 24); Eric, too, remarks on how pretty she is; only Mrs Birling seems to see nothing of value in her, preferring to view her strong character as 'giving herself ridiculous airs' (p. 46).

GRADE BOOSTER

When you are writing about characterisation, you should not only describe how a character looks and behaves, but also the other ways in which an author constructs their identity. Eva Smith provides a good opportunity to explore more subtle characterisation: consider how this absent character is developed and evaluate how she works, not just as a character but also as a dramatic device.

Key quotation

The Inspector: 'This afternoon a young woman drank some disinfectant, and died, after several hours of agony, tonight in the infirmary.'
(p. 17)

Her horrible death, described so graphically by the Inspector, will shock and horrify any audience, especially as Priestley ensures that our first impressions of her are positive. For instance, Birling tells the Inspector that she was a good worker and she was clearly someone who spoke up for herself and her fellow workers.

Strong character though she is, she is also presented as vulnerable. The Inspector tells us that she had no parents or home to go back to, no savings from the low wages she earned, and so was easily taken advantage of by men. She moves steadily down the social ladder, whereas those who exploit her are poised to move in the opposite direction. But the more of a victim she is portrayed as being, the more principled she becomes: being 'gallant' (p. 38) when Gerald finishes their relationship, and refusing to marry Eric because he does not love her. Priestley demonstrates her moral superiority to Eric when she discovers that the money he gives her is stolen and refuses to accept any more.

Eva is an everywoman: perhaps Priestley chose her surname Smith as the epitome of one of the faceless crowd, her identity merging with the masses in the Inspector's final speech, invoking us all to recognise the millions of Eva and John Smiths we are bound to if society is to hold together. Eva's story allows us to reclaim those faces and those names, but by keeping her off stage Priestley cleverly reminds us that these people remain marginalised, and largely unthought-of by the ruling classes. Until, that is, something goes wrong.

Edna

Edna is a minor character, appearing very briefly in the play. Her most noticeable appearance is to introduce the Inspector, and it is fitting that this is done by a working-class character. Some productions, such as Stephen Daldry's recent interpretation, have invested the character with greater significance than the script suggests, but perhaps her main role is to remind us that England is deeply hierarchical, and we can better see that when we are able to compare and contrast the wealth of the Birlings with not only the exploited and absent Eva Smith, but also with those, like Edna, who are struggling at the bottom of the class system. For Priestley, it is the Ednas of the world who need equality of opportunity as much as the Eva and John Smiths.

GRADE FOCUS

Grade 5
To achieve Grade 5, students will develop a clear understanding of how Priestley uses language, form and structure to create characters, supported by appropriate references to the text.

Grade 8
To achieve Grade 8, students will examine and evaluate the ways Priestley uses language, form and structure to create characters supported by carefully chosen and well-integrated references to the text.

Build critical skills

To what extent is Edna comparable to Eva? Do you think the Birlings exploit both, or is one more fortunate – and less oppressed – than the other?

REVIEW YOUR LEARNING

(Answers are given on p. 102.)

1 How is Mr Birling described by Priestley in the first stage directions?

2 How does Mr Birling describe himself when speaking to Gerald and the rest of his family?

3 What literary device is used by Priestley to allow the audience to know more about events than the characters do?

4 How is Mrs Birling described by Priestley when we first meet her?

5 What is Mrs Birling's worst 'crime'?

6 How is Sheila described at the beginning of the play?

7 In what ways do Eric and Sheila change over the course of the play?

8 What name does Eva Smith adopt when she meets Gerald?

9 What connotations does the Inspector's name have, and why might this be important?

10 What do Eva and Edna have in common?

Themes

Target your thinking

- What are themes and why are they important in a play? (**AO1**, **AO3**)
- What are the main themes of *An Inspector Calls*? (**AO1**, **AO3**)
- Why are themes so important in *An Inspector Calls*? (**AO1**, **AO3**)

In literature, a theme is an idea that a writer explores through language, form and structure. A theme raises questions in the minds of readers or audience members. It is something that the writer wants you to think about and it might appear in an examination question as 'ideas about...' In some instances, writers may hope that as a result of thinking about a particular theme, the reader may change their attitudes and even their behaviour.

For some, all the characters in *An Inspector Calls* are merely vehicles for Priestley's own political views and, as such, they lack any real subtlety. This is a matter of personal opinion, but it might be worth considering that if this were completely true then it is unlikely that the play would have remained so popular for so long: audiences need to connect with those they watch on stage, and although we undoubtedly do engage with ideas, at a deeper level we also want to empathise and sympathise with the characters who bring those ideas to life. Audiences like to suspend disbelief and connect with characters on stage as human beings. It is also possible to be aware of different interpretations of key themes in the text.

There are several different ways of categorising the themes in *An Inspector Calls*, and some inevitably overlap. Here is a suggested list of the main themes:

- Appearance and reality
- Morality and the law
- The relationship between the sexes
- Responsibility and community
- Power and class.

Appearance and reality

The conflict between appearance and reality is one of the most important themes in the play: it can be found in every act and, to varying degrees, each character seems to struggle with distinguishing between what *appears* to be real and what actually is real. Priestley uses dramatic irony to develop the many conflicts between appearance and reality, thus ensuring that the audience is often aware of the gap between them. That said, not everything is revealed to the audience, and part of the play's on-going appeal is that it remains a mystery. And of course, when the final curtain comes down the audience is left thinking about how much of what they have just seen is a straightforward domestic drama and how much is something more metaphysical, featuring a supernatural 'inspector' compelling the characters to undergo an endless cycle of recriminations before finally accepting their collective responsibility.

Act One begins with a long description of the Birlings' dining room. It is worth re-reading these **stage directions** and beginning to think about how important appearance and reality are. Priestley is very specific about the impression he wants to convey to the director, and to the audience. Look at the following extract from the stage directions.

> 'At the moment they...are celebrating a special occasion, and are pleased with themselves.'
>
> (p. 2)

In this statement appearance is at odds with reality, and the same will go for much of the rest of the play. For instance, although the Birlings are marking a special occasion (the engagement of Sheila and Gerald), the reality will soon be very different: instead of celebrating love they will soon be faced with a horrible death. The alcohol on the table will not be used to toast the couple, but to dull the pain of the revelations. The trappings of affluence, the props on stage that articulate joy and optimism, will soon seem hollow. The sudden shift in mood, from one of joy to one of bitterness and recriminations, adds to the emotional power of the action.

Outwardly the Birlings and Gerald appear prosperous ('heavily comfortable'), but note that Priestley also adds that this is not a 'cosy' nor a 'homelike' (p. 1) place. Instead, it has weight and gravity; like its owner, Mr Birling, the house is 'heavy-looking', 'portentous', 'provincial' (p. 1). Even the light conveys a growing conflict in the mood: it begins as something pink and intimate but once the Inspector starts questioning them it is closer to a spotlight: bright, hard, interrogating, unforgiving. But does it illuminate? Does it tell us the truth? To 'throw some light' on to something should make it clear, but the reality is more clouded than that in this play. Notice, for example, that just after the Inspector's arrival is announced Mr Birling says: 'Give us some more light' (p. 10), but it takes the whole play before we get a better insight into what really happened, and the final telephone call at the end of Act Three returns us again to something darker, more shadowy.

Stage directions: the instructions given by the author to the director and the cast about how to stage a production; this might range from advice on lighting, to props, to how the actors might want to portray the characters.

GRADE BOOSTER

```
As a student
of English
Literature
your focus
should be on
Priestley's
language, his
characteris-
ation, and
the themes
and ideas he
explores.
You should
always keep
in mind his
stagecraft,
however: how
the play works
on stage has
been carefully
thought about,
and looking
at his stage
directions —
such as those
on the set
design — give
you a further
insight into
his thinking.
```

Key quotation

Mrs Birling: (reproachfully) 'Arthur, you're not supposed to say such things.'
(p. 2)

Build critical skills

Look at the rest of Mr Birling's speech: where else is there a conflict between appearance and reality?

Key quotation

Gerald: 'We've no proof it was the same photograph and therefore no proof it was the same girl.'
(p. 67)

The Birlings and Gerald seem, initially at least, happy and successful and at ease with each other's company. Gerald seems to be a loving fiancé but in actual fact he has cheated on Sheila; Eric appears high-spirited but in reality has a problem with alcohol. We soon learn that much of the outward success is a facade, concealing events and actions that are much darker (even Alderman Meggarty is revealed to be 'one of the worst sots and rogues in Brumley', p. 35).

Mrs Birling in particular has a high regard for appearances and for what she deems correct behaviour, while having behaved disgracefully towards a desperate young woman.

This important theme is evident in many other areas too. For instance, Mr Birling's long speech in Act One, in which he looks forwards to peace and prosperity, suggests that all is well in Europe, when this was patently not the case.

Key quotation

Mr Birling: 'That's what you've got to keep your eye on, facts like that, progress – and not a few German officers talking nonsense and a few scaremongers here making a fuss about nothing.'
(p. 7)

But nowhere in this speech is the conflict between appearance and reality more effectively symbolised than in Mr Birling's description of the *Titanic* as being 'absolutely unsinkable' (p. 7). That ship symbolises very well that no matter what appearances we construct and what precautions we take to avoid disaster, real life has a habit of wrecking them.

But appearance and reality are most obviously in conflict when we consider Eva Smith herself. She appears to be a young woman who, because of how she is treated by the Birlings and by Gerald, finds herself in a desperate situation, unable to find a way out other than through taking her own life.

The tension between this narrative and other possibilities, however, means that the reality is not so clear: what if Gerald is right and the picture shown to each character is of a different girl? How would we feel as an audience if we thought that there was no suicide, and that the Inspector was indeed a fake? Would that make any difference? How would that change how we judge the Birlings? Or are Eric, Sheila

▲ The *Titanic* setting sail in 1912

and the Inspector right in claiming that it makes no difference and that we have to accept we 'are members of one body' (p. 56)? Such points are worth exploring because they lead us to consider the very complex ideas associated with Priestley's writing.

Morality and the law

A key idea in the play is the question of morality. This is a play that seems to have clearly marked lines between right and wrong. If we agree with Priestley's argument then we end the play in no doubt that the Birlings and Gerald contributed to Eva's death. The Inspector makes this unambiguous just before he leaves in Act Three:

> 'Each of you helped to kill her. Remember that. Never forget it.'
>
> (p. 55)

He then judges each of the characters, condemning them, in differing degrees of severity, for the morality of their actions and each, in turn, accepts what he says, much like condemned prisoners accept the sentence passed down to them by a judge.

GRADE BOOSTER

There are many ways of interpreting the Inspector: some see him as Priestley's representative on stage, others as a supernatural being from the future. But it is also possible to see him as not just an Inspector, but also as judge and jury, all wrapped up in one complex character. Look closely at the Inspector's judgements of each character: are they all fair? To what extent are your views of each character's actions influenced by the Inspector?

There are also suggestions in the play that Birling sees himself as above the law because of his position and the fact that he plays golf with the Chief Constable. He attempts to intimidate the Inspector:

> 'Perhaps, I ought to warn you that he's an old friend of mine, and that I see him fairly frequently.'
>
> (p. 16)

Of course, none of the characters actually *does* anything illegal; yes, their actions might have been selfish, immoral, spiteful and even reckless – but not illegal. For example, it was legal for Mr Birling to pay his workers as little as possible, but was it the moral thing to do?

Build critical skills

Once you have finished your first reading of the play, think about how many other examples you can find where appearance does not match the reality. What do you think was Priestley's intention in creating these differences?

Build critical skills

Eric's stealing of money was, for him, not theft because he planned to return it to his father; furthermore, he took it to support Eva when she needed it. Was that a moral act? She refused to take it. What might that suggest to the audience?

Build critical skills

Priestley cleverly blurs the boundaries between what is lawful and what is morally right. But why does he do it?
- Is he arguing that we should act morally, even if that means we step outside the law? If so, what are the implications of such an attitude?
- Is he arguing that through collective responsibility many of the crimes people are forced to commit would not occur? If so, how realistic is that?
- Is he arguing something else? Consider the whole text, and focus very carefully on the Inspector, when thinking about these difficult ideas.

The relationship between the sexes

The relationship between the sexes is central to *An Inspector Calls*. There are four female characters (Sheila, Mrs Birling, Edna and Eva), but only Sheila and Mrs Birling have lengthy speaking parts, Edna has only 24 words in the play, and Eva – central though she is – does not appear at any point. Contrast this with the male characters and it could be argued that this is a play written by a man about a **patriarchal society** that oppresses working-class women and marginalises all women, regardless of status. But how valid is such a view?

It is interesting to note that Priestley chooses a woman to be the victim in the play. Perhaps this was because in order to gain audience sympathy he needed his victim to be as vulnerable as possible. There was no welfare state in 1912 and so there were few opportunities open to a working-class woman like Eva if she lost her job. Many turned to prostitution just to survive.

The 'sowing of wild oats' by young men such as Gerald and Eric was tolerated, although not talked about in polite society, but it would have been unthinkable for a middle-class young woman such as Sheila to be anything other than chaste.

The choices open to girls like Sheila were only marginally better than for Eva. They were not expected to work. Their purpose in life was to find a rich, respectable husband, which partly explains the joyous celebration of the engagement party as the play opens.

In 1912, a woman was still considered the possession of her husband or father. Middle-class women were seen as delicate flowers and protected from the harsher realities of life, which is why Birling tells his daughter to 'Run along' (p. 17) when the Inspector is speaking about Eva. Even Mrs Birling, however, has been protected from outside affairs as she is

Patriarchal society: a society run by men and in the interests of men, and in which positions of power are traditionally filled by men rather than women.

unaware that men visit prostitutes in the town or that her son has a drink problem.

There was change in the air, however, as the play is set at a time when women were campaigning for the vote and for greater equality. Mrs Birling seems blissfully unaware of this and has accepted completely the traditional role of an Edwardian wife and mother. There are signs, however, that Sheila has been in some ways influenced by the Suffragettes. Although she appears submissive and superficial at the beginning of the play, she gradually shows a more independent spirit, insisting on being present, on having her say and choosing to break off the engagement.

▲ Suffragettes campaigning for the vote for women

The relationship between the male and female characters is never stable; indeed, the tensions between Mr and Mrs Birling, Eric and his mother, the Inspector and each of the female characters, Sheila and her father, as well as, of course, the male characters' relations with Eva, are never far from the surface.

Perhaps the relationship that undergoes the biggest change is that between Sheila and Gerald. The announcement of their engagement is the reason the characters are assembled in the Birling home at the start of the play. At first, they appear very happy: Sheila shows excitement

Build critical skills

Think about the relationships between the characters: who do you think has the least healthy relationship, and who do you think has the healthiest? What do you think are Priestley's aims in presenting them in this way?

when Gerald produces the ring. 'Oh – Gerald – you've got it – is it the one you wanted me to have?' (p. 5). What does this reveal about their relationship?

Sheila flirts with him about port, and asks her mother to drink to their health. But it does not last: indeed, within a few minutes of the beginning of the play Sheila mentions how 'all last summer' Gerald 'never came near' her (p. 3). We later learn that this was because he was having an affair with Eva Smith. The relationship between Sheila and Gerald is a facade, and by the beginning of Act Two it is seriously under threat. Even though Sheila says that she respects Gerald for his honesty about Eva, their engagement ends bitterly.

Other relationships between the sexes are also troubled: Mr and Mrs Birling are introduced by Priestley as belonging to different classes, and we are told that Mrs Birling is rather 'cold' (p. 1). These characteristics can be seen in how she treats her husband (criticising him at the start of Act One for being socially awkward), and also in how they argue and accuse each other in Act Two (p. 45).

Both Gerald and Eric have sexual relations with Eva, but apart from short-term financial support they do not provide for her nor protect her from the difficulties of being a young, unemployed woman. Indeed, it could be argued that they exploit her. The same could be said of others, for example Mr Birling treats Eva so callously that even Eric thinks that it was 'a dam' shame' (p. 16).

Although it is possible to see class as playing a greater role in the destiny of each character than gender, Priestley seems to be arguing that the two cannot be separated: Eva dies because she was an uneducated – but not unprincipled – working-class woman who was easily exploited by middle-class men. She has very limited options once she is sacked by Milwards, and there are suggestions that she turns to prostitution in order to survive. Her fate would have been different if she had been a working-class man or a middle-class woman. Of course, Eva is not the only working-class female character in the play: Edna, the maid, represents the servant class that was so widespread in the Edwardian age.

GRADE BOOSTER

In writing about theme in the examination, you need to be aware of the question that is being asked, and you need to show that you have thought deeply about it. You do not need to come up with a definitive answer.

Priestley seems to be pessimistic, both about the position of women in society and about the relationship between the sexes; but there is hope, residing mostly in Sheila, but also in Eric. It is they who show they are

Key quotation

Gerald: 'Why on earth don't you leave us to it?'

Sheila: 'Nothing would induce me...'

(p. 34)

Build critical skills

To what extent is Eva exploited by the male characters? Is she a helpless victim who has no say in her fate, or is she a willing partner in her relationships with both Gerald and Eric? Are Gerald's and Eric's intentions any different from Alderman Meggarty's?

able to change. And it is Sheila who is alert and sensitive enough to the Inspector's message to understand the full implications of what he is accusing the Birlings of doing. Indeed, it is the relationship between the Inspector and Sheila, which bears similarities to that between teacher and student, that allow us to see something different and more constructive developing in the future because it has, at its heart, shared values and a strong sense of mutual respect.

GRADE **BOOSTER**

> Works of literature are rarely entirely optimistic nor totally bleak. It is important to show that you understand that, although Priestley identifies the darker aspects of humanity, he also, through the characters like the Inspector, Sheila and Eric, and through Eva's principled, selfless behaviour, indicates how a more socially responsible society could be created.

Responsibility and community

For Priestley, the Birlings and Gerald are all, to varying degrees, responsible for Eva's death. For Mr Birling, those who believe that 'everybody has to look after everybody else' are 'cranks'; for him, 'community' is 'nonsense', an invention that reduces everyone to 'bees in a hive' (p. 10), all working for each other, with personal ambition subsumed under the general good. For Priestley, and for socialists, it is only through accepting collective responsibility that we can truly state that we are all free, and free from the exploitation and repression of ruthless bosses who are motivated purely by self-interest and 'lower costs and higher prices' (p. 4). The collective good creates a fairer society, where there might indeed be fewer Birlings, but where there will also be fewer Eva and John Smiths.

GRADE **BOOSTER**

> Make sure that you have a clear understanding of the differences between a socialist view of society and a capitalist view of society: complex though these terms are, a clear grasp of how Mr Birling's views are very different from Priestley's will help you to make sense of the political messages of the play.

But understanding that all characters are responsible for Eva's death is only part of the picture: what is important to consider is which characters fully understand and accept responsibility for their own actions. After all, society can change only if there is a willingness to change from within. It is here where, in an otherwise bleak play, we find hope.

Build critical skills

Priestley seems quite clear about who is responsible for the death of Eva Smith. For him, and for the Inspector, it is the Birlings and Gerald who are guilty of this crime. But to what extent is this true? Does Eva contribute to her own death in any way? Does society in general influence her fate?

Build critical skills

Why do you think the Inspector admits that the young are often more easily impressed, and whom do you think he means by 'we'?

Key quotation

Mr Birling: 'I must say, Sybil, that when this comes out at the inquest, it isn't going to do us much good. The Press might easily take it up–'
(p. 45)

There are three characters in the play who clearly see the need to accept responsibility for one's own actions: the Inspector, Sheila and Eric (we could also include Eva in this, but that is not so clear). Importantly, it is only Eric and Sheila who change their views radically over the course of the play and, as noted in the previous section, it is no coincidence that both belong to a younger generation. Mrs Birling notices the change in her daughter when she says: 'You seem to have made a great impression on this child, Inspector' (p. 30). And it is clear that this is part of the Inspector's intentions: he replies, 'coolly', that 'We often do on the young ones. They're more impressionable' (p. 30).

Mr and Mrs Birling do not accept responsibility for their actions; instead, they are more concerned with how the scandal might affect their reputations. In Act Two Mr Birling, on hearing that Mrs Birling had rejected Eva's plea for help, admits that the impact on the family might be serious.

Neither character shows any regret over their actions and they never apologise. Even Mrs Birling, when convinced that the Inspector is a hoax, seems unmoved by the implications of what she has done, even challenging Sheila, when her daughter asks sarcastically if they all intend to carry on as if nothing has happened, by asking 'why shouldn't we?' (p. 71). Gerald appears to emerge the least damaged: Sheila respects him a little more than she did at the beginning, and even the Inspector admits that he 'at least had some affection for her [Eva] and made her happy for a time' (p. 56). It is Gerald, however, who acts most methodically in constructing an alternative interpretation of the events; he is motivated partly out of a desire to find out the truth, but also to escape responsibility.

We could claim that, for Priestley, Eva does not seek to avoid responsibility, and this is most clearly shown when she rejects Eric's stolen money and refuses to consider marrying him because she realises he does not love her. She is reported throughout the play as behaving in a dignified manner, and this is at odds with the behaviour of her social 'superiors'.

Eva Smith, like Eric and Sheila, belongs to the 'famous younger generation' (p. 72); they might not, in the words of Mr Birling, be able to 'take a joke' (p. 72), because they know that the things he finds trivial or amusing are very serious. In many ways a definition of being mature is understanding when to take something seriously, and to know where your responsibilities lie. It does not matter how old you are – in fact, Priestley shows us that age is not always an indicator of wisdom.

Power and class

Power manifests itself in many aspects of *An Inspector Calls*. It could be argued that each character's treatment of Eva is an assertion of their power over someone weaker than themselves. While a feminist might see this power imbalance in terms of gender, a socialist would define each of these exchanges as essentially class-based. The Birlings and Gerald exploit Eva because they belong to a different, more powerful class and in order for their power to be maintained and extended they have to ensure that movements between classes are not extensive or disruptive.

The irony is that arguably the most powerful and prejudiced character in the play is the only character who has moved from one class to another: Mr Birling. He is 'rather provincial in his speech' (p. 1) and has married his 'social superior' (p. 1). To some extent this makes his treatment of Eva even more unforgivable. Priestley drops subtle hints that Birling is not, naturally, of the same class as the rest of his family and Gerald: thanking 'cook', as his wife says, exposes his awkwardness with the finer aspects of social etiquette.

Birling abuses his power, as do all the other characters in the play (even, it could be argued, the Inspector), but they do not do this only with Eva. Mr and Mrs Birling threaten and patronise Eric and Sheila, often reducing them to children rather than the adults they are; it could even be argued that the Inspector himself uses his massive presence, as well as the authority that goes with his post, to intimidate and undermine each character he questions. The difference between him and the Birlings is that he is aware not only of his responsibility, but also of the real meaning of his duty to others. His use of power is as a means to an ends, whereas too often with the Birlings it is handed out without thinking beyond what serves their own self-interests.

> **Build critical skills**
>
> To what extent does Priestley present Eva as completely without fault? Is this your view, or do you think his representation of her avoids idealisation?

> **Build critical skills**
>
> Why do you think Priestley created Mr and Mrs Birling as being from different classes? What was his aim, and what do you think this added dimension to their characterisation, and to their relationship, brings to the play?

> **Key quotation**
>
> *The Inspector: 'Public men, Mr Birling, have responsibilities as well as privileges.'*
> (p. 41)

GRADE *FOCUS*

Grade 5

To achieve Grade 5 students will reveal a clear understanding of the key themes of the play and of how Priestley uses language, form and structure to explore them, supported by appropriate references to the text.

Grade 8

To achieve Grade 8 students will be able to examine and evaluate the key themes of the play, analysing the ways that Priestley uses language, form and structure to explore them. Comments will be supported by carefully chosen and well-integrated references to the text.

REVIEW YOUR LEARNING

(Answers are given on p. 103.)

1 What is a theme?

2 What are stage directions?

3 How does the lighting alter to reflect the changing mood of the play?

4 How does the *Titanic* symbolise the conflict between appearance and reality?

5 Who does the Inspector blame for killing Eva Smith?

6 What do the Birlings and Gerald do that is against the law?

7 What was the name of the group of women who campaigned for equal rights for women?

8 Which relationship between two characters undergoes the biggest change (and why)?

9 Which two characters in the play accept responsibility for their actions and learn from this experience?

10 Why does Eva not agree to marry Eric?

Language, style and analysis

Target your thinking

- How does Priestley use setting in *An Inspector Calls*? (**AO2**)
- How does Priestley use stage directions? (**AO2**)
- What are the main language techniques used by Priestley? (**AO2**)

You will notice from the questions above that, when analysing language and style, the Assessment Objective with which we are most concerned is AO2, which refers to the writer's methods. This is usually highlighted in the exam question by the word 'how'. Language and style are of vital importance since they are the medium through which writers help to create our understanding of plot, character and themes.

Examiners report that AO2 is often the most overlooked objective by students in the examination. For example, candidates who fail to address AO2 often write about the characters in a play or novel as if they were real people involved in real events rather than analysing them as 'constructs' or creations of the writer.

To succeed at AO2, you must deal effectively with the writer's use of language, form and structure.

Form

Very simply, the form of *An Inspector Calls* is that of a play. There are certain dramatic conventions associated with the play form, which we might term stagecraft. These encompass style, stage directions, sets, stage props, lighting, costume and, of course, dialogue. The decisions that a playwright makes about all these different aspects are closely related to both the structure and the language of the play. Turn to page 26 for analysis of the structure of *An Inspector Calls*.

Style

An Inspector Calls is a very popular play for a number of reasons, but perhaps the main reason is simple: it tells a compelling story that has a powerful moral message. It remains relevant to any society that suffers from injustice. Another reason why it maintains its popularity, however, is that it is very well written: Priestley's use of language, the style the play was written in and also its structure, distinguishes it as a superbly crafted piece of drama in which all its parts contribute to its unforgettable climax.

The style is interesting because at first it appears to be a form of 'whodunnit', a play involving the revelation of a death at the beginning, followed by an investigation that eventually reveals the culprit. This was a popular dramatic form at the time the play was written. As the play develops, however, it moves closer in form to a medieval morality play, with a strong message about the importance of community and responsibility.

Stage directions

Obviously, when watching the play on stage, the audience is not aware of what is in the stage directions. Stage directions are there to help an actor or a reader to interpret what might be going on, to mark exits and entrances, to indicate a particular action by a character, to show how the playwright might want the actor to deliver a particular line or to make clear what the playwright might have wanted in terms of lighting or props.

Priestley's use of stage directions is unusually detailed and specific. Sometimes they are there simply to indicate action, such as 'Birling lights his cigar and Gerald, who has lit a cigarette, helps himself to port, then pushes the decanter to Birling' (p. 8), although even this apparently neutral direction could be seen to suggest something about the cosy, masculine solidarity that exists between the two businessmen.

Sometimes stage directions are there to suggest how a particular line should be read. For instance, on page 16, Birling speaks 'rather angrily' and Eric replies 'sulkily'.

Other stage directions are there to help the actors to express the build-up of tension. For example, near the end of the play, Gerald rings the infirmary to enquire whether any suicides have been brought in that day. The stage direction reads:

> *'As he waits, the others show their nervous tension. Birling wipes his brow, Sheila shivers, Eric clasps and unclasps his hand, etc.'*
>
> (p. 70)

Priestley's precise stage directions pinpoint important actions in order to reveal deeper truths. In the opening stage directions, Priestley tells us that Mr Birling sits at one end of the table and his wife sits at the other end. While this could be interpreted as an indication of the formality of their lifestyle, it could also be a visual metaphor for the lack of closeness in their relationship.

Similarly, although Sheila and Gerald ought to be behaving like young lovers, their conduct at the start of the play seems forced and awkward. We find out very soon in Act One that Gerald had neglected Sheila the previous summer, and Sheila's tone, although outwardly friendly, is twice described by the author as 'half playful, half serious' (p.3). That tension is not entirely dispelled even when Gerald gives her the engagement ring she longed for, as her kiss is only 'hastily' (p. 5) done.

The comparatively few props that are used encourage the audience to focus on the words and actions of the actors. Clearly, for Priestley *An Inspector Calls* is a play where the message is of utmost importance. It is a play in which the audience needs to concentrate above all on what is being said on stage.

The set

Stage props

This is a **domestic drama** set wholly within one room, perhaps symbolising the enclosed world of the Birlings and introducing the themes of the play with no distractions. The atmosphere and time period are established as soon as the curtain goes up on Act One: Priestley describes the Birlings' home as being a 'fairly large suburban house', with 'good solid furniture of the period.' We are in their dining room to celebrate the engagement of Sheila Birling and Gerald Croft. Priestley is precise in his stage directions, offering advice to a director should a realistic set be used, but offering other practical suggestions should the 'tricky business' (p. 1) of re-setting the scene be too difficult to overcome.

The audience will immediately recognise that the Birlings are affluent. Everything about them and their house conveys an impression of the 'heavily comfortable', and this is reinforced not just by the furniture but by other props we see on stage: dessert plates, champagne glasses, a decanter of port, a cigar box. The telephone, placed on its own table to show it off, is an important but subtle reminder of the outside world. It does not ring until the end of the play, when it is key to the resolution of the action. It is another symbol of luxury as only the wealthy had telephones in 1912.

Domestic drama: a play that is largely or wholly staged in the characters' home and that focuses on the everyday concerns of a certain class, or classes, of people in that society.

▲ Eric (played by Edward Hammond) in the 1973 Mermaid Theatre production

The sense of a room that is impressive but not homelike reflects the tensions between the characters that can be discerned from the opening exchanges, and that become explosive once the Inspector begins to investigate them: why does Mr Birling choose to confide in Gerald, but not in his own son, about his possible knighthood? Why are Gerald's parents not present for the engagement of their son to Sheila (do they disapprove of him marrying below himself)? What was Gerald doing last summer when he hardly saw Sheila? Why does Eric guffaw suddenly when Gerald promises to be careful from now on (does he know something we don't?)? Why is Eric so nervous, and why is he drinking so much? Such tensions, although hinted at in the script, are made visible on stage through the set, and they hold our attention from the outset.

Lighting

The lighting 'should be pink and intimate', a soft flattering colour to disguise the family's ugly behaviour, perhaps suggesting their cosy rose-tinted lifestyle. When the Inspector arrives, however, the lighting 'should be brighter and harder', denoting a change and suggesting an interrogation room, not a family room. This attention to detail might appear rather confining to a reader, but for a theatre audience it works subtly and effectively.

Costume

The figures on stage are dressed in evening dress, 'the men in tails and white ties, not dinner jackets' (p. 1) indicating wealth, status and formality. Only Edna, the parlourmaid, is dressed differently and reminds us that this is not a world without hierarchy or, inevitably, tensions.

Dialogue: the direct speech of characters involved in conversation.

Received Pronunciation (or RP): the standard accent of Standard English in the United Kingdom; sometimes referred to as 'BBC English'; it has a neutrality relative to other British regional accents and is an accent in itself that is often associated with those in positions of power.

Dialogue

When looking at the language in a play, we are principally concerned with **dialogue**. Dialogue can be used in a number of ways, including to move the action forward, to reveal character, to create humour, pathos or atmosphere, and to introduce and develop themes.

Generally, the dialogue in *An Inspector Calls* is accessible and easy to understand. It is mostly in **Received Pronunciation**, as appropriate to the social status of the characters, although we are also told that Birling is 'rather provincial in his speech' (p. 1) to suggest he is of a lower social class than his wife. Priestley, keen to ensure that his message is clear, does not use any difficult or obscure words. The dialogue is also, to some extent, naturalistic.

For example, characters often 'cut in' or interrupt each other. If you listen to conversations in your own family, you will realise that this is a normal feature of speech. In the play, Priestley uses this technique in different ways. By the Inspector it is used to establish authority and take control. For example, while the Birlings are all arguing about who is to blame for Eva's death, the inspector interrupts them:

> The Inspector: *(taking charge, masterfully)* 'Stop!'
>
> (p. 55)

On the other hand, Priestley also uses it to show Eric challenging his father. For example, when Birling says that the smaller gathering makes speech making more difficult, Eric interrupts him with:

> 'Well don't do any...'
>
> (p. 4)

Dashes are used to indicate natural speech patterns and pauses, for instance with Birling, who is speaking 'rather heavily' (p. 6). At other times they are used to indicate emotional upset:

> Sheila: *(rather distressed)* 'Sorry! It's just that I can't help thinking about this girl – destroying herself so horribly – and I've been so happy tonight...'
>
> (p. 17)

In addition, the dialogue includes incomplete sentences – again, a feature of normal conversation:

> Birling: '...And look at the way the auto-mobile's making headway – bigger and faster all the time. And then ships...'
>
> (p. 7)

Irony

Dramatic irony – used by the playwright when the audience are aware of something that a character might not be – is used a great deal by Priestley and involves many of the characters. Very obvious examples are Birling's misplaced optimism about there not being a war and about labour troubles being a thing of the past, examples which are humorous to most audiences. Mrs Birling's scathing condemnation of the father of Eva's child, which turns out to be her own son, however, is used to create tension and high drama.

Irony is an effective tool used by writers to show up gaps between appearance and reality (see 'Themes', p. 40), and it can be used in more than one way. For example, consider this short extract in the light of what you know about each character at the end of the play:

> Sheila: *(half serious, half playful)* 'Yes – except for all last summer, when you never came near me, and I wondered what had happened to you.'
>
> Gerald: 'And I've told you – I was awfully busy at the works at that time.'
>
> Sheila: *(same tone as before)* 'Yes, that's what *you* say.'
>
> (p. 3)

Build critical skills

Analyse Priestley's use of naturalistic dialogue in the following short extract and explain what the effect on the audience might be:

Mrs Birling: *(very distressed now)* 'No – Eric please – I didn't know – I didn't understand–'

Eric: *(almost threatening her)* 'You don't understand anything. You never did. You never even tried – you–'

Sheila: *(frightened)* 'Eric, don't – don't–'
(p. 55).

Build critical skills

There are several examples of Priestley's rather dry sense of humour in the play: locate them, and think about how they affect the atmosphere of the moment, as well as our interpretation of a character. Why would Priestley use humour, however lightly, in a play this serious?

Proleptic irony: a device used by playwrights to anticipate an event that will occur later in the play.

This is an example of **proleptic irony**: we only realise how significant this is when we hear about Gerald's affair with Daisy Renton in Act Two. Similarly, in Act One, Gerald states 'You seem to be a nice well behaved family–' (p. 8), when of course the opposite is true, as will be revealed in the course of the play.

Language and character

The language used by each of the characters is appropriate to their personality, and there is little padding: the conversations are usually direct, either developing our understanding of the plot, of the context or, more usually, of the person speaking.

Mr Birling

In Act One Priestley establishes Mr Birling's dominance before the arrival of the Inspector through the length of Birling's speeches as he uses **rhetorical devices** to lecture his family and Gerald. For example, he combines long, complex sentences addressing global issues, such as the possibility of war and civil unrest, with short, direct sentences to make his personal views clear and unambiguous. These speeches suggest to us a confident man, who is sure of his stance and regards others' views as 'silly', a man of whom it might be said that he enjoys the sound of his own voice. He talks down to the young men, calling them 'you youngsters' (p. 7) and 'my boy' (p. 9).

Rhetorical devices: techniques used in public writing and speaking to make the message more effective and memorable.

Hyperbole: the deliberate use of exaggeration for effect.

However, the **hyperbolic** vocabulary used in Act One, for example 'There'll be peace and prosperity and rapid progress everywhere–' (p. 7), never returns after the Inspector challenges his authority.

But in a play that is so preoccupied with appearance versus reality, and where so many of the characters are exposed as hypocrites and liars, we have to look beyond the surface reality of the conversations. Birling's early speeches, slow and weighty though they are, are also demonstrably wrong, and we judge him accordingly. He is the character who is most associated with Priestley's use of dramatic irony, a technique he uses to suggest that Birling is a fool and therefore likely to be wrong on other matters too.

Sheila and Eric

Sheila begins the play with very little of any real importance to say. She seems more interested in the ring she receives than in the man who gives it to her. Her use of contemporary slang to Eric – 'squiffy' (p. 3) and 'chump' (p. 5) – perhaps suggests someone who is a little frivolous, maybe even immature. Eric seems equally shallow (or drunk), uttering empty, clichéd, phrases such as 'we'll drink their health' (p. 4), 'all the best…Good old Sheila!' (p. 5) and 'steady the buffs!' (p. 5). Both characters, however, representing as they do the younger generation, quickly become symbols of hope: as they develop, so does their use of language, and so in turn do the ideas they begin to explore.

Eric, in particular, asks a good many questions and in this sense speaks for the audience. Sometimes, this is to provide us with essential information:

> Eric: 'Is that why she committed suicide? When was this, Father?'
>
> (p. 13)

Sometimes, his questions are used to establish a difference between himself and his father. He asks if war is possible, and he also challenges his father's decision to sack Eva Smith:

> 'He could have kept her on instead of throwing her out. I call it tough luck'
>
> (p. 15)

Sheila, even more than her brother, quickly adopts a social conscience that is retained to the end of the play, and her vocabulary reflects this. It is she who reacts emotionally. The word 'horrible' (p. 45) is repeated when she refers to the pregnant Eva's suicide and she refers to the family's actions as 'crimes' (p. 63) to which they were made to 'confess'.

Mrs Birling

Priestley reflects Mrs Birling's preoccupation with correctness by making her speech patterns generally the most formal of the characters'. Her prudish nature is reflected by the use of the word 'disgusting' (p. 38) to describe Gerald's affair with Eva, and the fact that she cannot bring herself to use the word 'pregnant' to describe Eva's condition. Her snobbish views are reflected by her use of the phrase 'a girl of that sort' (p. 47) to describe Eva.

Her composure is only broken when Eric challenges her, when her syntax breaks down ('No – Eric – please – I didn't know – I didn't understand–', p. 55).

Gerald

Gerald's language suggests he is polite, charming and deferential at the start of the play: 'Absolutely first class' (p. 2). His words on Eva's dismissal, 'You couldn't have done anything else' (p. 15), suggest he shares Birling's values and attitudes.

Priestley presents him as unwilling at first to share his story: 'All right, if you must have it' (p. 34). At only one point do his emotions overwhelm him, and both stage directions and syntax reflect this:

> Gerald: *(distressed)* 'Sorry – I – well, I've suddenly realised – taken it all in properly – that she's dead.'
>
> (p. 35)

Build critical skills

Sheila: '…But he made us confess.'

Mrs Birling: 'He certainly didn't make me confess – as you call it…' (p. 60).

Comment on Priestley's use of language here and on its effect on the audience.

This soon passes, and he quickly recovers, speaking 'steadily' (p. 36) and 'gravely' (p. 39), and his calm presence of mind continues until the end of the play.

The Inspector

The Inspector rarely speaks in long sentences. His lines are short, sharp and to the point. He does not immediately reveal his purpose and this clearly throws the other characters off balance.

> Mr Birling: 'Well what can I do for you? Some trouble about a warrant?'
>
> The Inspector: 'No, Mr Birling.'
>
> Birling: *(after a pause, with a touch of impatience)* 'Well, what is it then?'
>
> (p. 11)

At other times, Priestley shows the Inspector using graphic language to hammer home the horror of Eva's fate:

> Inspector: *(very sternly)* 'Her position now is that she lies with a burnt out inside on a slab...'
>
> (p. 46)

Metaphor: a comparison where something is spoken of as if it were something else.

Oratory: the art of formal speaking.

Polysyndeton: the repeated use of conjunctions for emphasis and effect.

Emotive language: the use of words deliberately to provoke a strong response from the audience.

His most famous speech, at the end of the play, is when his naturalistic dialogue changes into something more passionate, more like the speech of a great orator. Here, his is the language of the disappointed teacher, the angry parent, the prophet from the future, the priest listening to a confession, the politician with an agenda for social improvement, the crowd-pleasing rhetorician who is seeking a response – from another character or the audience. He is most likely to use **metaphor** to make more vivid his message ('We are members of one body...and...the time will soon come when, if men will not learn that lesson, then they will be taught it in fire and blood and anguish', p. 56). This controlled **oratory**, complete with **polysyndeton** and strong **emotive language**, confirms the political – and polemical – aspect of the play.

For this reason, some argue that the Inspector is Priestley's mouthpiece – simply a vehicle for the playwright's beliefs in social justice.

Build critical skills

'One Eva Smith has gone – but there are millions and millions and millions of Eva Smiths and John Smiths still left with us, with their lives, their hopes and fears, their suffering and chance of happiness, all intertwined with our lives, and what we think and say or do.' (p. 56).

How does Priestley make the Inspector's words effective for the audience?

GRADE FOCUS

Grade 5

To achieve Grade 5, students will show a clear appreciation of the methods Priestley uses to create effects for the reader, supported by appropriate references to the text.

Grade 8

To achieve Grade 8, students will explore and analyse the methods that Priestley uses to create effects for the reader, supported by carefully chosen and well-integrated references to the text.

REVIEW YOUR LEARNING

(Answers are given on p. 103.)

1 What is a domestic drama?
2 What is dialogue?
3 Why might a director want Gerald and all of the Birlings (except Mr Birling) to speak with Received Pronunciation?
4 Why might Priestley have the Inspector use graphic language to describe Eva's death?
5 Why does Sheila's language change over the course of the play?
6 What is stagecraft?
7 What is dramatic irony?
8 How does Priestley suggest that Birling talks down to the young men?
9 What is oratory?
10 What word does the prudish Mrs Birling avoid using?

Tackling the exams

Target your thinking

- What sorts of questions will you have to answer?
- What is the best way for you to plan your answer?
- How can you improve your grade?
- What do you have to do to achieve the highest grade?

Your response to a question on *An Inspector Calls* will be assessed in a 'closed book' English Literature examination. This means that you are not allowed to take copies of the examination text into the examination room. Different exam boards will test you in different ways and it is vital that you know on which paper the twentieth century drama text will be, so that you can be well prepared on the day of the examination.

Whichever board you are studying, the following table explains in which paper and section the play appears and gives you information about the sort of question you will face and how you will be assessed.

Exam board	AQA	Edexcel	Eduqas	OCR
Paper and section	Paper 2, Section A: Modern prose or drama	Paper 1, Section B: Post-1914 British drama or fiction	Component (Paper) 2, Section A: Post-1914 prose/drama	Paper 1, Section A: Modern prose or drama
Type of question	Students will answer one essay question from a choice of two on their studied modern prose or drama text.	Students have a choice of two questions on their chosen post-1914 British fiction or drama text. There is a short quotation from the text to help students think about the question.	Students will be assessed on an extract-based question in Section A. There will be one question on *An Inspector Calls* in this section.	Part (a) is a comparative analysis based on one extract from *An Inspector Calls* and a thematically linked unseen modern, same-genre extract. Part (b) requires students to explore 'another moment' from their set text linked to the theme of Part (a).
Closed book?	Yes	Yes	Yes	Yes

Exam board	AQA	Edexcel	Eduqas	OCR
Choice of question?	Yes	Yes	No	No
Paper and section length	Paper 2: 2 hours 15 minutes. Section A approx. 50 minutes.	Paper 1: 1 hour 45 minutes. Section B 50 minutes.	Paper 2: 2 hours 30 minutes. Section A approx. 45 minutes.	Paper 1: 2 hours. Section A: part (a) 45 minutes; part (b) 30 minutes.
Percentage of whole grade	20%	25%	20%	25%
AOs assessed	AO1 AO2 AO3 AO4	AO1 AO3 AO4	AO1 AO2 AO4	AO1 AO2 AO3
Is AO4 (SPaG) assessed in this section?	Yes	Yes	Yes	No

Marking

The marking of your response will vary depending on the board your school or you have chosen. Each exam board has a slightly different mark scheme, consisting of a ladder of levels. The marks you achieve in each part of the examination will be converted to your final overall grade. Grades are numbered from 1 to 9, with 9 being the highest.

It is important that you familiarise yourself with the relevant mark scheme(s) for your examination. After all, how can you do well unless you know exactly what is required?

Assessment Objectives for individual assessments are explained in the next section of the guide (p. 72).

Approaching the examination question

First impressions

First, read the whole question and make sure you understand *exactly* what the task requires you to do. It is very easy in the highly pressured atmosphere of the examination room to misread a question – and this can be disastrous. Under no circumstances should you try to twist the question to match the one that you spent hours revising or the one that you did brilliantly on in your mock exam! The best advice will be familiar, but it is given by so many teachers to their students because it is true: answer the question.

How to read the question

Are you being asked to think about how a character or a theme is being presented? Make sure you know so that you will be able to sustain your focus later.

Look carefully at any bullet points you are given. They are there to help and guide you.

The four boards that offer *An Inspector Calls* as a text have very different styles to their questions: the structure, as well as the language used, needs to be carefully considered, and you need to prepare for these elements very carefully. Attempting questions in the style of those you will get in the examination itself is an essential part of the revision process.

Edexcel

Your response will be marked for the range of appropriate vocabulary and sentence structures, and accurate use of spelling and punctuation.

The Inspector: Each of you helped to kill her.

(Act Three)

To what extent did all of the characters help kill Eva Smith?

You must refer to the context of the play in your answer.

[40 marks]

[8 marks for the range of appropriate vocabulary and sentence structures, and accurate use of spelling and punctuation]

Important: Always be aware of the Assessment Objectives that your exam board is assessing. For Edexcel AO2 is **not** assessed in this question.

What is the main focus for this question? Clearly, you are being asked about the theme of **responsibility**, but it is also worth noting the phrase 'to what extent', which is asking you to evaluate each character's guilt. You will also note that this style of question refers to the **context** of the play; in this case it is important to show that you understand the wider issues Priestley was writing about (such as socialism and capitalism, and social class conflicts). Underline these key words before you answer the question as they will help you plan your response.

A choice of two questions will be given for Edexcel. Below you can see examples of the question types from other exam boards, which have been annotated in this way.

AQA

How and *why* does *Eric change* in *An Inspector Calls?*

Write about:

- how Eric responds to his family and the events of the play
- how Priestley presents Eric by the way that he writes.

[30 marks]

[AO4: 4 marks]

Or

How does Priestley explore the *conflict between generations* in *An Inspector Calls?*

Write about:

- the ideas about generational conflict in *An Inspector Calls*
- how Priestley presents these ideas by the way he writes.

[30 marks]

[AO4: 4 marks]

Eduqas

You should use the extract below and your knowledge of the whole play to answer this question.

Write about the *character* of *Arthur Birling* and the way he is *presented* in *An Inspector Calls*.

In your response you should:

- refer to the extract and the play as a whole
- show your understanding of characters and events in the play.

[40 marks]

[5 marks for accuracy in spelling, punctuation and the use of vocabulary and sentence structures]

Mr Birling: I'm delighted about this engagement and I hope it won't be too long before you're married. And I want to say this. There's a good deal of silly talk about these days – but – and I speak as a hard-headed business man, who has to take risks and know what he's about – I say, you can ignore all this silly pessimistic talk. When you marry, you'll be marrying at a very good time. Yes, a very good time – and soon it'll be an even better time. Last month, just because the miners came out on strike, there's a lot of wild talk about possible labour trouble in the near future. Don't worry. We've passed the worst of it. We employers at last are coming together to see that our interests – and the interests of capital – are properly protected. And we're in for a time of steadily increasing prosperity.

Gerald: I believe you're right, sir.

Eric: What about war?

Mr Birling: Glad you mentioned it, Eric. I'm coming to that. Just because the Kaiser makes a speech or two, or a few German officers have too much to drink and begin taking nonsense, you'll hear some people say that war's inevitable. And to that I say – fiddlesticks! The Germans don't want war. Nobody wants war, except some half-civilised folks in the Balkans. And why? There's too much at stake these days. Everything to lose and nothing to gain by war.

OCR

You may have noticed from the earlier table that the OCR question format is very different from the other boards, in that part (a) requires students to write a comparative answer based on two extracts, one from *An Inspector Calls* and the other from a modern same-genre text. There are examples of this form of question given on the OCR website.

Spot the differences!

- Only Eduqas provides an extract from the play to refer to.
- Only Eduqas does not assess AO3.
- Only Edexcel refers directly to 'contexts' in the question.
- Only Edexcel does not assess AO2.
- AQA and Edexcel each offer a choice of two questions.
- Only OCR does not assess AO4 in this section.
- Only OCR uses an unseen extract for comparison.

Approaching the AQA and Edexcel questions

Both boards offer a choice of questions on *An Inspector Calls*. Before choosing which question to answer, read them both carefully and make sure you understand exactly what the tasks require you to do. An important word in the AQA questions is likely to be 'how', which means that Priestley's methods will be crucial in your response. Think very carefully before deciding which question to attempt. Choose the question that gives you the best chance to impress the examiner with your depth of knowledge.

Approaching the Eduqas question

First, read the passage very carefully, trying to get an overview or general impression of what is going on, and what or who is being described.

Now read the passage again, underlining or highlighting any words or short phrases that you think might be related to the focus of the question and are of special interest. For example, they might be surprising, unusual or amusing. You might have a strong emotional or analytical reaction to them or you might think that they are particularly clever or noteworthy.

These words or phrases may work together to produce a particular effect or to get you to think about a particular theme or to explore the methods the writer uses to present a character in a particular way for their own purposes. You may pick out examples of literary techniques such as use of imagery or contrast, or sound effects such as alliteration or a particularly clever use of stagecraft. You may spot an unusual word order, sentence construction or use of punctuation. Don't forget to consider the effect of stage directions, if included, as well as dialogue. The important thing to remember is that when you start writing you must try to **explain the effects** created by these words or phrases, or techniques, and not simply identify what they mean. Above all, ensure that you are answering the question.

Approaching the OCR question

For part (a) of the OCR question all of the above advice holds true, but remember you are **comparing two extracts** from different texts. Look for similarities and differences in the ideas and themes in each extract and in the ways they are presented by the writers. This might seem like a lot to do but it is suggested that you spend 45 minutes on part (a). Part (b) is closer in style to an AQA- or Edexcel-style question but you are asked to focus on only one 'moment' from *An Inspector Calls* rather than the play as a whole.

Planning your answer

It is advisable to write a brief plan before you start writing your response to avoid repeating yourself or getting in a muddle. A plan is not a first draft. You will not have time to do this. In fact, if your plan consists of any full sentences at all, you are probably eating into the time you have available for writing a really insightful and considered answer. Managing your time effectively – including planning time – is essential to writing a good exam essay.

A plan is important, however, because it helps you to gather and organise your thoughts, but it should consist only of brief words and phrases. It should work for *you*, rather than be written in great detail to impress the examiner.

You may find it helpful to use a diagram of some sort – perhaps a **spider diagram** or **flow chart**. This may help you keep your mind open to new ideas as you plan, so that you can slot them in. Arranging your thoughts is then a simple matter of numbering the branches in the best possible order. Or you could make a list instead. The important thing is to choose a method that works for *you*.

The other advantage of having a plan is that if you run out of time, the examiner can look at the plan and may be able to give you an extra mark or two based on what you were about to do next.

Writing your answer (AQA, Edexcel and Eduqas)

And they're off…

Now you are ready to start writing your answer. The first thing to remember is that you are working against the clock and so it's really important to use your time wisely.

It is possible that you may not have time to deal with all of the points you wish to make in your response. It is important to keep the focus of the examination question in your mind as you write: keep returning to those underlined words and phrases in the question. If you simply identify several language features or a handful of themes and ideas and make a brief comment on each, you will be working at a fairly low level. The idea is to **select** the ones that you find most interesting and to develop them in a sustained and detailed manner. In order to move up the levels in the mark scheme, it is important to write a lot about a little, rather than a little about a lot.

You must also remember to address the **whole question** as you will be penalised if you fail to do so.

Part of exam technique is making sure that the examiner knows that you are developing an argument. You can make this clear by using 'signal words' to signpost your argument.

If you have any time left at the end of the examination, do not waste it. Check carefully that your meaning is clear and that you have done the very best you can. Look back at your plan and check that you have included all your best points. Is there anything else you can add? Keep thinking until you are told to put your pen down.

Referring to the author and title

You can refer to Priestley either by name (make sure you spell it correctly) or as 'the writer'. You should never use his first name (John) or his initials (J.B.) – this sounds as if you know him personally. You can also save time by giving the play title in full the first time you refer to it, and afterwards simply referring to it as 'the play'.

GRADE **BOOSTER**

Do not lose sight of the author in your essay. Remember that the play is a construct — the characters, their thoughts, their words, their actions have all been created by Priestley — so most of your points need to be about what he might have been trying to achieve. In explaining how his message is conveyed to you (for instance through an event, something about a character, use of symbolism, personification, irony and so on) don't forget to mention his name.
For example:

- Priestley makes it clear that…
- It is evident from…that Priestley is inviting the reader to consider…
- Here, the reader may well feel that Priestley is suggesting…

The more a student refers only to characters' names, rather than to the author, the more likely they are to lose sight of the author's intentions. This can result in losing a lot of marks because the essay will lack the evaluative, critical insight that is often found in very strong essays.

Writing in an appropriate style

Remember that you are expected to write in a suitable **register**. This means that you need to use an appropriate style. This means:

- *not* using colloquial language or slang, e.g. 'Birling is a really horrible man.' (The only exception is when quoting directly from the text.)
- *not* becoming too personal, e.g. 'Mrs Birling is a really disgusting woman and I hate her.'
- using suitable phrases for an academic essay, e.g. 'It could be argued that…', not 'I reckon that…'
- *not* being too dogmatic – don't say 'This means that…'; it is much better to say 'This might suggest that…'.

You are also expected to be able to use a range of technical terms correctly. If you can't remember the correct name for a technique but can still describe its effect, you should still go ahead and do so.

The first person ('I')

It is perfectly appropriate to say 'I feel' or 'I think'. You are being asked for *your* opinion. Just remember that you are being asked for your opinion about *what* Priestley may have been trying to convey in his play (his themes and ideas) and *how* he does this (through the characters, events, language, form and structure of the play). Very often you simply do not need to use 'I': writing phrases such as 'It is clear that…' or 'The audience might view this…' often conveys a more mature and sophisticated style.

Spelling, punctuation and grammar (AO4)

Spelling, punctuation and grammar are targeted for assessment by AQA, Edexcel and Eduqas in this section. Therefore you have to take particular care not only with your ideas, but also with how accurately you express them. Take time to plan your work, but also to check it to ensure that you correct errors that will lose you marks. Think about the key literary terms that are frequently misspelled (such as 'simile', 'imagery', 'characterisation') and make every effort to get them right. If the examiner cannot understand what you are trying to say, they will not be able to give you credit for it.

How to raise your grade

The most important advice is to answer the question that is in front of you, and to start doing so promptly. When writing essays in other subjects, you may have been taught to write a lengthy, elegant introduction explaining what you are about to do. In the Literature examination, though, you have only a short time so it is best to get started as soon as you have gathered your thoughts together and made a brief plan.

Students often ask how long their answer should be. It is difficult to give a definitive answer because clearly the size of candidates' handwriting differs, and quality is always more important than quantity. A strongly focused answer of two or three sides that hits the criteria in the mark scheme is perfectly able to be rewarded at the very highest level. Conversely, if a response is six or seven sides long but is not focused on the question, it will not receive many marks at all.

Sometimes students panic because they don't know how to start. It is absolutely fine to begin your response with the words, 'In this extract Priestley presents…' if it is a passage-based question (Eduqas or OCR).

If it is a more traditional 'essay-style' question (AQA or Edexcel), then address the question directly: for example, 'The conflict between generations is a central theme in *An Inspector Calls*, and Priestley uses it not only to show how misguided the older generation are, but also, through the younger characters, to offer some hope for the future to the audience.'

If you are responding to an extract, or extracts, begin by picking out interesting words and phrases and unpicking or exploring them within the context or focus of the question. For example, if the question is about the way that responsibility is presented, you need to focus on picking out words and phrases related to this theme, and then on building a set of connected ideas that could form the foundation for a coherent argument.

If you are following AQA, Eduqas or OCR, it is crucial that you deal effectively with the methods used by the writer and the effects created by them. What methods has the writer used? Although there is a whole range of methods with which you need to be familiar, it might be something as simple as a powerful adjective. What do you think is the impact of that word? It might be that the word you are referring to has more than one meaning. If that's the case, the examiner will be impressed if you can discuss what the word means to you, but can also suggest other meanings.

Remember that if you are following the AQA, Edexcel or OCR specifications your knowledge of context (AO3) is also assessed. Would Priestley's initial audience have viewed things differently from a modern audience, given that the play was first performed in a shattered Europe soon after the end of World War II and at the start of the founding of the welfare state in Great Britain?

Be very careful to avoid lapsing into narrative. If you are asked about how Priestley presents Birling, remember that the focus of the question is about the methods that Priestley uses. Do not simply tell the examiner what Birling does or what he is like; this is a very common mistake.

If you are entered for Eduqas remember you also have to deal with the focus of the question in the play **as a whole**. You will be penalised if you do not do this so you *must* leave time. If you feel you have more to offer in terms of comments on the extract, leave a space so that you can return to it if necessary.

> GRADE **BOOSTER**
>
> It is important to make the individual quotations you select brief and to try to *embed* them. This will save you time, enabling you to develop your points at greater depth and so raise your grade.

Key points to remember

- Do not just jump straight in. Spending time wisely in the first moments may gain you extra marks later.
- Write a brief plan.
- Remember to answer all parts of the question.

- If your question is extract-based (Eduqas) then focus on the *details* in the passage in your answer and remember you must also refer to the play as a whole.
- Use your time wisely. Try to leave a few minutes to look back over your work and check your spelling, punctuation and grammar, so that your meaning is clear and so that you know that have done the very best that you can.
- Keep an eye on the clock.

GRADE FOCUS

Grade 5
- Candidates have a clear focus on the text and the task and are able to 'read between the lines'.
- Candidates develop a clear understanding of the ways in which writers use language, form and structure to create effects for readers.
- Candidates use a range of detailed textual evidence to support comments.
- Candidates use understanding of the idea that both writers and readers may be influenced by where, when and why a text is produced.

Grade 8
- Candidates produce a consistently convincing, informed response to a range of meanings and ideas within the text.
- Candidates use ideas that are well linked and often build on one another.
- Candidates dig deep into the text, examining, exploring and evaluating the writer's use of language, form and structure.
- Candidates carefully select finely judged textual references that are well integrated in order to support and develop responses to texts.
- Candidates show perceptive understanding of how contexts shape texts and responses to texts.

Achieving a Grade 9

To reach the very highest level you need to have thought about the play more deeply and to have produced a response that is conceptualised, critical and exploratory at a deeper level. You might, for instance, challenge accepted critical views in evaluating whether the writer has always been successful. If, for example, you think Priestley set out to create sympathy for the poor, do you think is he as successful as is generally supposed?

You may feel that the creation of sympathy for the poor through what might be described as the blatant manipulation of the reader's or audience's emotional response to Eva Smith alienates some modern audiences, or you might feel that Priestley's overtly political position is too didactic. Exploring such issues, and evaluating their success, is something a top-grade candidate would be able to do successfully and objectively.

You need to make original points clearly and succinctly and to convince the examiner that your viewpoint is really your own, and a valid one, with constant and careful reference to the text. This will be aided by the use of short and apposite (really relevant) quotations, skilfully embedded in your answer along the way (see 'Sample essays', p. 78).

REVIEW YOUR LEARNING

(Answers are given on p. 104.)

1 Will you be assessed on spelling, punctuation and grammar in your response to *An Inspector Calls*?
2 Can you take your copy of the play into the exam?
3 Why is it important to plan your answer?
4 What should you do if you finish ahead of time?
5 What advice would you give to another student about using quotations?

Assessment Objectives and skills

All GCSE examinations are pinned to specific areas of learning that the examiners want to be sure candidates have mastered. These are known as Assessment Objectives or AOs. If you are studying *An Inspector Calls* as an examination text for AQA, Eduqas, Edexcel or OCR, the examiner marking your exam response will be trying to give you marks, using the particular mark scheme for that board. All mark schemes, however, are based on fulfilling the key AOs for English Literature.

Assessment Objectives

The Assessment Objectives that apply to your response for *An Inspector Calls* depend on the exam board, as shown below.

Exam board	AQA	Edexcel	Eduqas	OCR
AOs assessed	AO1 AO2 AO3 AO4	AO1 AO3 AO4	AO1 AO2 AO4	AO1 AO2 AO3
Is AO4 (SPaG) assessed in this section?	Yes	Yes	Yes	No

For AQA, Edexcel, Eduqas and OCR:

AO1 Read, understand and respond to texts. Students should be able to:
  - maintain a critical style and develop an informed personal response
  - use textual references, including quotations, to support and illustrate interpretations.

For AQA, Eduqas and OCR only:

AO2 Analyse the language, form and structure used by a writer to create meanings and effects, using relevant subject terminology where appropriate.

For AQA, Edexcel and OCR only:

> **AO3** Show understanding of the relationship between texts and the contexts in which they were written.

For AQA, Edexcel and Eduqas only:

> **AO4** Use a range of vocabulary and sentence structures for clarity, purpose and effect, with accurate spelling and punctuation.

(You can't forget about it entirely, but if your spelling or punctuation leaves something to be desired at least you can lift your spirits by reminding yourself that AO4 is only worth about 5 per cent of your total mark.)

What skills do you need to show?

Let's break the Assessment Objectives down to see what they really mean.

> **AO1** Read, understand and respond to texts. Students should be able to:
> - maintain a critical style and develop an informed personal response
> - use textual references, including quotations, to support and illustrate interpretations.

For AQA, Edexcel, Eduqas and OCR.

This AO tests your knowledge and understanding of the text you have studied; it also assesses your ability to express a clear opinion on the text within the context of the question. For example, if you were to write: '*An Inspector Calls* is about the Birling family's bad treatment of Eva Smith' you would be beginning to address AO1 because this is a **personal response**. Notice, however, that in the grade descriptors there is the inclusion of the adjective '**informed**' and this indicates that you have to have a strong understanding of the play to base your judgements on if you are to access the higher marks.

In order to do this you have to '**use textual references, including quotations, to support and illustrate interpretations**'. This means using short, carefully chosen quotations from the text. For example, if you wanted to show that the Birlings did treat Eva badly you could write that in Act Three the Inspector accuses all of them of being responsible for her death when he says 'each of you helped to kill her'. Alternatively, you could make close references to the text to support your points, writing that: 'It is clear that the Birlings are responsible for treating Eva Smith badly because in Act Three the Inspector accuses them all of killing her.'

Overall, most candidates do well in AO1. If you answer the question, and give evidence from the text to support you points, you will have nothing to worry about with this Assessment Objective.

> **AO2** Analyse the language, form and structure used by a writer to create meanings and effects, using relevant subject terminology where appropriate.

For AQA, Eduqas and OCR only.

AO2, however, is a different matter. Most examiners would probably agree that covering AO2 is a weakness for many candidates, particularly those students who only ever talk about the characters as if they were real people.

In simple terms, AO2 refers to the writer's methods and is often signposted in questions by the word 'how', e.g. in the phrase 'How does the writer present…'.

Overall AO2 is equal in importance to AO1 so it is vital that you are fully aware of this objective.

The word '**language**' refers to Priestley's use of words. Remember that writers choose words very carefully in order to achieve particular effects. They may spend quite a long time deciding between two or three words that are similar in meaning in order to create just the precise effect they are looking for. Priestley's use of language is frequently very precise, in order to pin down details and to tie together a complex plot with many different themes. But he also uses words deliberately ambiguously (such as the Inspector having the surname Goole): your job as a student of literature is to prove to the examiner that you understand the choices the writer makes, and their intended effects.

If you are addressing AO2 in your response to *An Inspector Calls* you will typically find yourself using Priestley's name and exploring the choices he has made.

AO2 also refers to your use of '**subject terminology**'. As you are analysing drama you will have to know the meaning of terms often associated with this genre (such as 'dramatic irony', 'dialogue', 'audience' and 'stage directions'), but you should also know more general terms, such as 'symbolism', 'metaphor', 'characterisation' and 'imagery' and be able to use them with confidence. Even if you cannot remember such terms in the examination, you can still gain marks from describing their effect in the play.

'**Structure**' refers to how the play is put together. Most obviously, *An Inspector Calls* consists of three acts, but it is more sophisticated than that suggests (see p. 26 in the 'Plot and structure' section for a more detailed evaluation of Priestley's use of structure). *An Inspector Calls* is a 'well-made play', which, as the term suggests, means that it is a finely crafted piece of theatre. Above all, it keeps the audience interested throughout, even though there is very little real 'action'. The climaxes that do occur come at the end of each act, ensuring that we want to stay to see what happens next.

There are many 'exits and entrances' – characters leaving the stage and then returning with new information – and each of these skilfully contributes not only to the plot, but to how the characters see themselves and each other (in other words, their characterisation).

'**Form**' refers to the genre of the play, and *An Inspector Calls* is far more than a carefully written play that keeps an audience amused. It borrows from other genres – such as 'whodunnits' and detective fiction – and, in the character of the Inspector, it has an other-wordly, mysterious element that adds a great deal to its appeal. See page 51 of the 'Language, style and analysis' section for a fuller discussion of the genre of the play.

AO2 is an essential Assessment Objective. If you are not fully aware of its importance you will not be able to achieve anything other than a very low grade because you simply will not be answering the question.

> **AO3** Show understanding of the relationship between texts and the contexts in which they were written.

For AQA, Edexcel and OCR only.

AO3 is not considered as important as AO1 and AO2, but it is still worth approximately 15 per cent of your final mark in the examination as a whole; remember, however, that AO3 is not assessed on the *An Inspector Calls* question if you are entered for Eduqas.

To cover AO3 you must demonstrate that you understand the links between a text and its context. When was it written? Why was it written? Whom was it written for? For a play such as *An Inspector Calls*, knowing about its background is crucial to understanding much of its power. For example, Mr Birling's speech in Act One refers to the 'absolutely unsinkable' *Titanic*: the importance of this reference would be lost without knowing how significant an event this was to Edwardian England. And there is, of course, a dual historical focus to the play: it is set in 1912, just two years before World War I; and it was first performed in 1945, immediately after the end of World War II. Once we realise this, the

Inspector's final speech in Act Three takes on much more significance. You can find out more about the context of the play in the 'Context' section on page 9 of this guide.

It is particularly important to remember that AO3 should deepen your reading of the text: it should not be simply inserted into your essay unless there is a clear link with the question. That said, it would be difficult to write a satisfactory response to a question on *An Inspector Calls* without showing that you are aware of the different contexts it was written in. Getting the balance right – so that you ensure you are writing primarily a literature rather than a history essay – will come with practice.

> **AO4**   Use a range of vocabulary and sentence structures for clarity, purpose and effect, with accurate spelling and punctuation.

For AQA, Edexcel and Eduqas only.

Even though AO4 is worth only 5 per cent of your marks for the GCSE, it is important to remember that by ensuring your meaning is clear and that your spelling, punctuation and grammar are as accurate as possible, you will not only boost your marks for this Assessment Objective, but will also gain marks in each of the other Assessment Objectives.

The examiner must be able not only to read every word you write, but also to understand your meaning. So: plan your work to ensure that there are as few mistakes and crossings-out as possible. Check your work to make your meaning as clear as you can. If your spelling, punctuation and grammar are so bad that your meaning is confusing, or if the examiner literally cannot read what you have written because of your poor presentation, then you will inevitably lose marks. This is where practising writing essays before the examination can be so valuable: it allows you to focus on those areas that you know need to be improved.

What you will not gain many marks for

You will **not** gain many marks if you do the following:

- **Retell the story.** You can be sure that the examiner marking your response knows the play inside out. You will, at times, have to refer to a certain point in the play, but that should be focused and brief. A key feature of the lowest grades is 'retelling the story'. Don't do it.
- **Quote long passages.** Quotations should support a point you are making. They should be short and, preferably, embedded (you can test how embedded they are by simply removing the quotation marks and seeing if the sentence still 'flows'). Using long quotations will lessen the impact of the point you are trying to make as it will be unclear to

the examiner which part of the passage you are referring to. One- or two-word quotations can often be much more effective than one or two lines.

- **Merely identify literary devices.** You will never gain marks simply for identifying literary devices, such as the use of a simile or metaphor. You can gain marks, however, by identifying these features, exploring the reasons you think Priestley has used them and offering a thoughtful consideration of how they might impact on the reader, as well as giving an evaluation of how effective you think they are. Make doubly sure that you spell these literary terms correctly: practise writing them out (and defining them) as part of your examination preparation.

- **Give unsubstantiated opinions.** You do have to give a personal response to the question, but this should be based on evidence from the text. For example, it will not help you to write about your own political views in relation to the Birlings or Eva Smith. Showing an understanding of socialism and the political issues involved in the play, however, could strengthen an answer (if this is directly relevant to the question you are answering, of course).

- **Write about characters as if they are real people.** Remember: characters are constructs, not real people. They are created by the author for a reason – to explore themes, to articulate ideas and emotions. Retain a 'critical distance' so that you show the examiner how aware you are of the writer's use of characterisation.

REVIEW YOUR LEARNING

(Answers are given on p. 104.)

1 What does AO1 assess?
2 What sort of material do you need to cover in order to address AO2?
3 What do you understand by the term 'AO3'?
4 Which exam boards assess AO4 for *An Inspector Calls*?
5 Which exam board specification are you following and what AOs should you be focusing on?

Sample essays

The question below is typical of an **AQA** question.

How and why does Sheila Birling develop new understanding in
An Inspector Calls?

Write about:

- how Sheila develops in relation both to her family and to the Inspector
- how Priestley presents Sheila's development by the ways he writes.

[30 marks]

[AO4: 4 marks]

You will see below extracts from exam responses from two students working
at different levels. They cover much the same points. If you look carefully,
however, you will be able to see how Student B takes similar material to that
of Student A, but develops it further in order to achieve a higher grade.

In addressing the first bullet point, both students consider how Sheila
changes; Student B, however, has a more secure knowledge of this aspect of
the text, and also goes much further in addressing the second bullet point.

Student A, who is likely to achieve Grade 5, begins like this:

In this answer I will consider how Sheila develops
a new understanding in 'An Inspector Calls'.
She starts the play as an innocent young girl
who is more impressed with money and success
than anything else. However, by the end of the
play she has changed a lot and this symbolises
how the young are the symbols of hope in the
play. We first meet Sheila at the start of the
play. She is pretty and young and Priestley
says that she is 'very pleased with herself'.
She is also excited because the party her father
is hosting is to celebrate her engagement to
Gerald Croft, who is a rich young man and this
symbolises the merging of two families rather
than love. But by the end of the play Sheila has
changed a lot and seems more grown up; in
fact only her brother, Eric, could be said to have
grown up as much as her. This is optimistic. It
shows she has developed a new understanding.

1 Not a good start. Don't
say what you're going to
say. Just do it!

2 Avoid
stating the
obvious.

3 Good use of an
embedded quotation.

4 Returns to the
question, if a little
clumsily.

Student B, who is likely to gain a Grade 8 or 9, begins like this:

With the exception of Eric and Sheila, all the characters in J.B. Priestley's 'An Inspector Calls' fail to learn from their mistakes and, as such, do not understand the implications of their actions. It is Sheila who develops a clear understanding of the Inspector's message and, as a result, her relationship with the rest of her family undergoes a profound change: she sees them as the Inspector (and the audience) sees them, and this 'frightens' her. Importantly, through his subtle characterisation and stagecraft, as well as his development of key themes, Priestley shows how knowledge of an issue does not always lead to an understanding of it. Sheila's character evolves, moving from 'being pleased with life' to confessing that they are all implicated in various 'crimes and idiocies'.

1 Good confident opening.

2 Addresses first bullet and uses embedded quotations effectively.

3 Addresses second bullet and makes a valid point.

4 Uses two embedded quotations, from beginning and end.

Both students then go on to discuss Sheila's character in more detail.

Student A continues:

Sheila's engagement to Gerald is really important: it represents not only the marriage of two people but the merging of Crofts Limited and Birling and Company. At the start of the play we see that Sheila is mostly concerned with herself and Gerald. When she hears of Eva Smith's death from the Inspector she says although it has 'distressed' her the real shame is that she had 'been so happy tonight'. Eva's death matters to Sheila only because it has ruined her night.

But Sheila isn't just a silly girl. She is a complex character. For example, 'half playful, half serious'. Eric also says that she has 'a nasty temper sometimes'. This temper ended up with her getting Eva Smith sacked from her job in the clothes shop and it could be argued that this started her journey to suicide.

1 Some insight into character.

2 Qualifies and supports.

Sheila responds differently to the other family members and the Inspector. Her relationship with her father is never very good and he talks down to her throughout the play, trying to protect her from the Inspector's questions, as well as the descriptions of Eva's death. He refers to her as a 'child' which shows how much he does not understand her. Importantly, Mr Birling is absent for much of Sheila's exchanges with the Inspector, and so misses what she says. Like Eric, Sheila represents the younger generation, and although these characters are not close at the start of the play by the end they share similar views. When Eric says that they are all guilty, and that they cannot have 'a nice cosy chat' now that the Inspector has gone, it is Sheila who says he is 'absolutely right'. They represent hope. Sheila understands Eric and his drinking, telling her mother that he is 'squiffy'. Her relationship with her mother is never close, but it is interesting to compare and contrast these two female characters over the course of the play: Sheila develops, and grows up, by accepting her role in Eva Smith's death; Mrs Birling who, like her husband, repeatedly calls Sheila a 'child', doesn't develop, and doesn't change her views of Sheila. To some extent it could be argued that we see how much Sheila has changed through comparing and contrasting her with other members of her family, especially Mrs Birling.

3 Good, supported AO2 comment.

This is a good development of Student A's response, and shows that he/she has a 'clear understanding' of the text. There are regular references to 'understanding', and what it means, although they are not always developed. There are other factors that stop Student A moving up to a higher band: too much of the writing is descriptive; quotations are not always confidently used.

A better response appears below. Student B is working at a Grade 8, with certain aspects pointing to Grade 9. Compare this with Student A's extract and see if you can see why one would be given a higher grade than the other.

Sheila does not gain a 'new understanding' in a single moment of revelation; instead, she observes the other characters, listens to what they say and, importantly, begins to reassess her own behaviour and her own values. In this sense it could be argued that she echoes the audience's shifting perception of the action. To some extent her growth, and the widening of her mind, symbolises for Priestley a process of political awakening that the Suffragettes exemplified at the end of the nineteenth and beginning of the twentieth centuries. Sheila, then, is not only a character who undergoes a deeper personal understanding, but she also becomes politicised by Eva's death.

This 'journey' would not have been possible, or believable, had it not been for Priestley's skilled characterisation: we do not doubt that she could have acted in this way, nor that she is capable of such change. Her decision to break off her engagement to Gerald exemplifies both how she changes and also how convincing Priestley makes it. What could have been a moment of simple, emotional confrontation develops into something more reflective and deeper: Gerald defends himself against Mrs Birling, claiming his affair was 'not disgusting', and by the end of the play perhaps emerges with some credibility intact. But Sheila also grows, and instead of simply condemning him, appreciates his honesty. She confesses that because of how he behaves she respects him 'more than I've ever done before.' Such a statement could only be made through understanding; and, importantly, we can believe it only because Priestley's characterisation is subtle enough to capture her changing values and her growing up.

1 Addresses question and develops point.

2 Interesting and intelligent point – could have been further developed.

3 Skilful and appropriate exploration of context.

4 Addresses second bullet, and use of appropriate literary term.

5 Excellent knowledge and understanding.

This is clearly writing at a very high level, and the student is beginning skilfully to evaluate not only the first but also the second (more difficult) bullet point: it is this sophisticated bringing together of both aspects of the question that is particularly impressive.

Student A now begins to write about Priestley's writing technique in developing Sheila:

1 Effectively addresses question.

> JB Priestley's writing shows Sheila as a very complex character. But at the start of the play she is selfish and innocent. However, by the end of the play she seems to have changed the most: she accepts responsibility for what she has done, and has told the others that they must never 'forget' what the Inspector has told them. Priestley develops Sheila through getting her to interact with other characters. We learn about her from what she says, but we also learn about her from what Priestley writes in his stage directions. For example, we find out early on that she can be 'half playful, half serious', and Priestley writes this twice. She shows a lot of emotions: 'bitterly', 'tensely', 'wildly' are all words that Priestley writes to describe her. From this we can see that she is very passionate.

2 Quotations support valid point.

There are some good points here, and the comments made about Priestley's stage directions are persuasively made, perceptive, and supported by good, succinct references to the text. There are, however, some limitations to the analysis: statements about characters 'interacting' with each other, or about Sheila showing 'a lot of emotions' and being 'very passionate', at times lose the critical distance that Student B has: such observations, although not incorrect, move too close to seeing Sheila as being a real person (rather than as a construct created by Priestley for effect), and also state things that are rather too obvious.

Student B next explores the main argument of his/her essay:

1 Effective use of short, embedded quotation.

2 Convincing, thoughtful argument.

3 Understanding of Priestley's methods and effects.

Part of this growing up springs from Sheila gaining a greater sense of social responsibility. We see this in a number of different episodes, and taken together they contribute to her development as a character. For instance, she moves quite quickly from being a rather flat character prone to giggling, flirting and behaving 'gaily' in Act One, into an accomplice of the Inspector's who is capable of asking questions such as 'Were you in love with her Gerald?', and 'Did you go and see her every night?', to reaching convincing conclusions about herself and Gerald ('You and I aren't the same people who sat down to dinner here'). Sheila's understanding goes beyond her parents' limited and self-motivated questions about who did what and whether such things might affect their reputations; in contrast, Priestley shows how she is able to accept her own involvement in Eva's death, and then to look for direct answers to complex moral questions. Cleverly, this not only develops her as a character, but it also provides another perspective on events, thus offering a different voice from the Inspector's but reaching the same conclusions. In this way her words, and his, are validated, but without either feeling forced together by the author. Such is Priestley's skill as a playwright.

Throughout this response the candidate sustains a highly developed, sophisticated and penetrating analysis. References to the text are always appropriate and succinct, and there is good and effective use of literary terms. The student uses a general vocabulary highly effectively, and shows a very developed understanding of the skill required to make a play work.

Student A now concludes his/her essay by returning to the character of Sheila, but also seeks to address context:

> Sheila is an important character in the play because she shows that it is possible to learn from your mistakes and to gain a new understanding. She symbolises the younger generation who, although about to go to war (the play is set two years before WW1 starts), might be able to build a better world than the one that Mr and Mrs Birling have created. And the fact that she is a woman shows that that hope might come not from men like Gerald and Mr Birling, but from the Suffragettes who were campaigning for more power for women at the time.

1 Clear conclusion with some addressing of context.

This is a satisfactory conclusion: Student A returns to the question and shows a developed sense of Sheila as not only a character capable of change, but also as symbolising an important element of the text. The reference to the war develops out of this important point, but it is worth noting that this is the only moment in the essay when the play is placed in a wider context: for this question it would have been advisable to make appropriate references to key issues relating to gender, specifically those affecting young women like Eva and Sheila.

Overall, Student A has a good understanding of the text; there is also a good response to the task itself, with a clear understanding of its main focus. There are, however, missed opportunities to give detailed textual references (only one quotation is used) and there are lapses in technique that weaken the initial critical response. There is also only a token contextualisation at the end of the essay. Overall this is a clear response, but it lacks the insight necessary to move beyond Grade 5.

Student B now concludes his/her essay:

> In conclusion it is impossible to separate the 'how' and 'why' from Sheila's new understanding: they are interconnected, and develop out of her growing awareness of herself as a young woman in a complex world. She understands anew why her mirror-image – Eva Smith – had no choices left other than to take her own life but, unlike her parents and those of

1 Convincing personal response.

2 An interesting interpretation that could be further explained.

the older generation, she learns about her own involvement in this tragedy. Why she develops this understanding depends on Priestley's own views: he clearly saw her generation – and gender – as a source of hope; but it also works dramatically as well: along with Eric she is able to continue the questioning once the Inspector has left the stage. This is significant because Priestley is arguing that for change to happen, and for society to avoid learning lessons 'in fire and blood and anguish' we have to have the convictions necessary to act free of force, regardless of whether there is a crime committed, or indeed an Inspector present. At the end of the play, Sheila is more serious and less pleased with herself, and Priestley's characterisation is subtle enough for that to happen naturally and convincingly. Because of this she remains one of the most interesting characters in the play, and perhaps the most important.

3 Thoughtful analysis of Priestley's intentions.

This is a highly effective ending to a very convincing argument. What is probably the most impressive aspect of the essay is that it retains a focus on both aspects of a demanding question: Sheila's developing understanding, and Priestley's technique, are evaluated equally because they cannot be separated. Context is lightly, but effectively, introduced, and quotations are used to support points where appropriate. This is a mature and convincing response that clearly covers all the criteria for a Grade 8 response and begins to move from Grade 8 towards a Grade 9.

The sample question below is typical of an **Eduqas** question.

You should use the extract below and your knowledge of the whole play to answer this question.

Write about the importance of community and the way it is presented in *An Inspector Calls*.

In your response you should:

● refer to the extract and the play as a whole

● show your understanding of characters and events in the play.

[40 marks]

[5 marks for accuracy in spelling, punctuation and the use of vocabulary and sentence structures]

Mr Birling: *(solemnly)* But this is the point. I don't want to lecture you two young fellows again. But what so many of you don't seem to understand now, when things are so much easier, is that a man has to make his own way – has to look after himself – and his family too, of course, when he has one – and so long as he does that he won't come to much harm. But the way some of these cranks talk and write now, you'd think everybody has to look after everybody else, as if we were all mixed up together like bees in a hive – community and all that nonsense. But take my word for it, you youngsters – and I've learnt in the good hard school of experience – that a man has to mind his own business and look after himself and his own – and –

We hear the sharp ring of a front door bell. BIRLING stops to listen.

Student A, who is aiming for a Grade 5, begins his/her response like this:

In the play 'An Inspector Calls' the idea of community is very important and I will be writing about how this theme is presented in the extract and in the play as a whole. In the extract Mr Birling is lecturing his son Eric and his daughter's fiancé Gerald about his views on the world. The audience have already heard Mr Birling's views dismissing the idea that there could be a war and going on and on about how the Titanic is 'absolutely unsinkable' so they know not to take his opinions that seriously.

1 No need to rephrase the question like this – much better to get straight to the point.

2 Fair comment but could be more appropriately expressed!

3 Appropriate textual support and some evidence of understanding of effect.

After a slow start, the response is beginning to focus on the extract and shows some understanding of the play's events. There is some support but, as yet, no real evidence of the writer's methods being considered.

Now compare that opening with this one by Student B, who is working at a higher level.

1 Good to get straight to the point.

2 Good textual detail from outside the extract.

3 Knowledge of the correct terminology.

> In the extract Mr Birling is delivering a post-dinner lecture to his son, Eric, and his potential son-in-law, Gerald Croft, in which he offers them his experience as a 'hard-headed, practical man of business'. Even at this early stage in the play, however, Priestley has already ensured that the audience will view Birling's opinions with considerable scepticism through the playwright's use of dramatic irony. Birling's dismissal of the possibility of war in a play set in 1912, alongside his repeated claims about the 'unsinkable' Titanic, mean that the 1945 audience would be likely also to distrust his views on 'community'.

4 Clear understanding of the effect of the writer's method.

This is an impressive opening in that it quickly establishes an overview of the extract, shows good awareness of writer and audience, and reveals detailed textual knowledge. At this early stage an examiner would probably already have recognised this as a potentially high-achieving candidate.

In the next sections of their responses both students focus on the extract itself and discuss what it reveals about the theme of community.

Student A continues in this way:

1 Clear focus on the idea of community in the passage with brief, well-embedded evidence from the text.

> In the extract Priestley makes it clear that Mr Birling has no time for the idea of 'community' as he refers to it as '...all that nonsense.' Mr Birling thinks that people who believe in community are just 'cranks' and that a man should put himself and his family first rather than thinking about helping out the weaker members of society. Priestley was a great believer in the importance of community and it is interesting that it is just at this point that the Inspector arrives at the house as he is a character with the opposite view on community from Mr Birling. In the stage direction the bell is described as being 'sharp' and it will shock the audience and prepare them for Mr Birling to meet his match.

2 Some comment on the effect created by Priestley's use of structure.

3 Comment on the effect created by the stage direction.

87

Student A is showing focus on the task and is now beginning to address AO2 by considering the effects created by Priestley in the extract.

Now compare the way in which Student B begins to analyse the extract:

Throughout the extract Priestley makes it clear that Mr Birling has no time for the idea of 'community', believing instead in the selfish dog-eat-dog world of business where a man must look after himself. Priestley presents Birling's views through his dismissive language as he refers to community as '...all that nonsense.' Birling is presented here as a man who has no understanding of the realities of the world, something that is emphasised by his simplistic belief that life now is 'so much easier'.

1 Thoughtful comment on a detail from the extract.

Furthermore, Mr Birling describes people who write about community as 'cranks', having already criticised the '...Bernard Shawses and H.G. Wellses' of the world. As a socialist, Priestley would probably have counted himself as one of these 'cranks' and at this point the audience would be viewing Mr Birling as an unsympathetic and selfish character.

2 Awareness of the effect on the audience.

The extract stresses Birling's philosophy that a man should put himself and his family first and it is no coincidence that Priestley chooses this moment to introduce the Inspector into the play, the 'sharp' sound of the doorbell cutting through Mr Birling's lecture and heralding the introduction to the audience of one of the 'cranks' that he has just been so dismissive about.

3 Understanding of Priestley's structuring of the action.

4 Explaining the effect of the stage direction.

Student B has continued to focus on the task and is beginning to offer thoughtful comments on details from the extract, as well as explaining the effects created by Priestley's form and structure.

In the following sections of their responses, both students consider how Priestley uses other members of the Birling family to examine the theme of community in the play.

Student A continues as follows:

Mrs Sybil Birling is like her husband as she also has no time for the idea of community. It is ironic that she is an important member of the 'Brumley Women's Charity Organisation', which is meant to offer help to women in distress, but Mrs Birling uses her power to turn down Eva's cry for help. Priestley presents Mrs Birling as a snob who doesn't believe that working-class people have feelings or morals. This is shown when she says that a girl 'of that sort' would never refuse money. Mrs Birling's committee should be protecting the weaker members of the community but instead she is shown to look down on ordinary people.

In contrast to their parents both Sheila and Eric have more sense of the importance of community and Priestley uses them and the way they change to symbolise hope for the future. Early in the play Eric is presented as having some sympathy with Eva Smith and her co-workers in Birling's factory. He stands up to his father and calls it a 'dam' shame' that Eva was sacked and even says, 'I'd have let her stay.' Sheila is also presented as someone who has a stronger sense of community and the audience often see her siding with the Inspector, especially when she challenges her father by saying: '...these girls aren't cheap labour — they're people.'

1. Fair comment, but remember to foreground the writer.

2. Brief quotation, well embedded.

3. Some understanding of Priestley's methods.

4. Points are well supported with textual detail.

In these two paragraphs Student A makes clear, well-supported points about the Birling family and their links to community. Priestley's methods need more explanation but, overall, an impression of a Grade 5 response is emerging.

Now look at how Student B takes similar points but develops them further:

1 Thoughtful response with well chosen textual support.

Priestley presents Sybil Birling as her husband's 'social superior' and her dismissal of the notion of community is shown by the writer to be harsh and bigoted. As a 'prominent' member of the 'Brumley Women's Charity Organisation' the audience might expect her to offer support to vulnerable members of the community and she claims to have done 'useful work in helping deserving cases'. Priestley shows the audience, however, that Mrs Birling abuses her power to turn down Eva's case, and her language reveals her prejudices about girls 'of that sort', who she believes lack 'fine feelings' and moral values. Furthermore, Priestley creates a sense of Mrs Birling being proud of her actions, with her repeated use of 'I' as she describes her influence on 'my' committee.

2 Interesting point on Priestley's use of language – might have been analysed more fully?

Priestley uses contrast and symbolism to emphasise the differences between the generations, making it clear to the audience that hope for a better and fairer future lies with the young. Both Sheila and Eric develop greater understanding of the importance of community and Priestley shows them both to be affected by the Inspector's warning of 'fire and blood and anguish...', as they are shown at the end of the play to be frightened by their parents' failure to learn anything from this experience.

3 Good knowledge of the play as a whole.

4 Continuing focus on the question.

Early in the play Eric is presented as having some sympathy with Eva Smith and her co-workers in Birling's factory. He stands up to his father and calls it a 'dam' shame' that Eva was sacked and even says, 'I'd have let her stay...', indicating some commitment to the notion of community. Despite the rather selfish first impressions she creates, particularly in the incident at Milwards, Sheila is also presented by Priestley as someone who has a stronger sense of the importance of equality when she challenges her father by saying: 'these girls aren't cheap labour — they're people', a sentiment perhaps undermined by the revelation of her vindictive behaviour towards Eva in the store.

5 Thoughtful observation showing good knowledge of the play's events.

Here we see Student B offering thoughtful and wide-ranging ideas, revealing a detailed knowledge of the play and beginning to achieve the criteria for a Grade 8.

In the following extracts both students consider the role played by Inspector Goole with regard to the theme of community, before bringing their responses to a conclusion. Compare their two conclusions carefully and decide which one is the more effective.

Student A continues:

Probably Priestley's most powerful device for exploring the importance of community is his use of the Inspector himself. Inspector Goole is presented as the complete opposite of Mr Birling as he sees community as important as he believes that we are all linked together and are responsible for each other. The Inspector can be seen as a mouthpiece for Priestley's views on the importance of community and this is brought out powerfully near the end of the play when he tells the Birlings about the 'millions and millions' of Eva and John Smiths who make up our society. In this speech Priestley cleverly reminds the audience of Arthur Birling's earlier speech when the Inspector makes the simple statement 'We are members of one body', which contradicts Birling's selfish views.

Overall, it is clear that community is an important theme of the play as Priestley uses all his characters to show the audience that everyone in society deserves equal respect.

1 Clearly understands Priestley's intentions.

2 Awareness of Priestley's careful structuring of the action.

3 Conclusion could offer a final point rather than this simple summary.

Despite a slightly weak conclusion, Student A's response is certainly clear and focused on the task. It reveals a solid understanding of characters and events in the play and offers some explanation of the effects created by Priestley. Although AO2 is perhaps a little weaker than AO1 here, the response fits the criteria required for a Grade 5.

Student B concludes:

> The creation of Inspector Goole is perhaps Priestley's most powerful device for exploring the importance of community. Critics have seen the Inspector as representing the conscience of the nation as well as recognising him as the mouthpiece for Priestley's socialist views. Whether we interpret the Inspector as a supernatural 'spectre' or 'ghoul', as Priestley's punning implies, or as a more traditional police inspector, it is clear that he represents the absolute opposite of Birling's selfish, capitalist beliefs. Goole's mission seems to be to teach the Birlings the importance of community and to recognise their responsibility to protect our vulnerable neighbours.
>
> The Inspector's belief in community is emphasised in the hyperbole of his final speech, in which he pleads the case for the 'millions and millions and millions' of Eva and John Smiths who need our support and protection. Priestley uses simple, short, direct statements throughout this speech to ensure that the key messages of the play are inescapable for the audience: 'We don't live alone. We are members of one body.' These words echo Birling's dismissive comments about community and 'bees in a hive' and make it clear that collective responsibility is the only way to avoid 'fire and blood and anguish.'

1 Some consideration of alternative interpretations.

2 Understanding of technical term, well supported.

3 Effective conclusion, returning to the extract and using well-chosen textual references.

Student B's answer is a thoughtful and convincing personal response. There is some analysis of Priestley's methods and effects created, and textual support is appropriately used throughout. Overall, the response fits the criteria required for a Grade 8.

Note: both responses would receive full marks for AO4.

Top ten

As your examination is 'closed book' you might find it helpful to memorise some quotations to use in support of your points in the examination response. See the 'Tackling the exams' section on page 60 for further information about the format of the examination.

You don't need to remember long quotations; short quotes that you can embed into a sentence will be more effective. If all else fails, as long as you can remember the gist of what the quotation relates to, you can use a textual reference.

Top ten characterisation quotations

The following quotations can be used as quick reminders of the way that Priestley presents key elements of the main characters.

Mr Birling

'Mr Birling is a heavy-looking, rather portentous man in his middle fifties [and] rather provincial in his speech' (p. 1)

1

- 'Portentous' means pompous and self-important: there is a heaviness to him. Unlike the Inspector, though, his words do not carry weight: instead, he is slow and ponderous, and the description of his accent also marks him out as being of a lower class than the rest of his family.

'We hard-headed practical business men must say something sometime. And we don't guess – we've had experience – and we know' (p. 7)

2

- Mr Birling has a very high opinion of himself and his experience, but throughout the play we see his judgements about individuals, as well as about politics, exposed as misplaced.

'A man has to mind his own business and look after his own – and–' (p. 10)

3

- Mr Birling advocates that our priorities lie with ourselves, not with other people; importantly, this speech is interrupted by the arrival of the Inspector.

Mrs Birling

4 '[Mrs Birling] is about fifty, a rather cold woman and her husband's social superior' (p. 1)

- These stage directions highlight not only Mrs Birling's emotional coldness, but also her class. Class plays an important role in this play, and even in the Birlings' marriage there is potential class-based tension.

Sheila

5 'Sheila is a pretty girl, in her early twenties, very pleased with life and rather excited' (p. 1)

- The play begins with an engagement, and Sheila's excitement about her prospects are clear to see; but Priestley suggests, in his description of her being 'very pleased with life', that she is complacent and out of touch with the harsh realities of experience.

6 'But these girls aren't cheap labour – they're people.' (p. 19)

- This quotation shows that even early in the play Sheila has some sympathy for others.

Eric

7 'Eric is in his early twenties, not quite at ease, half shy, half assertive.' (p. 2)

- Although similar in age to his sister, Eric is less comfortable in company and, as we shall see, this springs from a number of issues: his drinking, his difficult relationship with his parents and, of course, his recent experiences with Eva.

Gerald

8 'Gerald Croft is an attractive chap, about thirty, rather too manly to be a dandy but very much the well-bred young man-about-town.' (p. 2)

- Here Priestley emphasises Gerald's sophistication and his age, which are both important as he will later on, in challenging the Inspector's story, prove himself to be more experienced, and more pragmatic, than the Birlings. The description of him being 'well-bred' is a reference to his social class.

Inspector Goole

'The Inspector…creates at once an impression of massiveness, solidity and purposefulness. He is a man in his fifties…He speaks carefully, weightily' (p. 11)

9

- The stage directions clearly identify the key characteristics of the Inspector: he conveys an air of importance, of seriousness, and thoughtfulness. Although similar in age to Mr Birling, their behaviour – in what they say, and how they act – could not be more different.

'I've thought that it would do us all a bit of good if sometimes we tried to put ourselves in the place of these young women counting their pennies in their dingy little back bedrooms' (p. 19)

10

- For some critics the Inspector's voice is sometimes very close to Priestley's own; here we can see the character moving beyond his role as a police inspector investigating a crime: there is a social conscience to his questions and observations that forces the other characters, and the audience, to sympathise with Eva Smith.

Top ten thematic quotations

Appearance and reality

Mr Birling: 'That's what you've got to keep your eye on, facts like that, progress – and not a few German officers talking nonsense and a few scaremongers here making a fuss about nothing' (p. 7)

1

- This 'nonsense' and 'fuss about nothing' is nothing of the sort, as evidenced by the outbreak of World War I in 1914.

Mr Birling: 'The *Titanic* – she sails next week…New York in five days – and every luxury – and unsinkable, absolutely unsinkable' (p. 7)

2

- The *Titanic* appeared to be impregnable, but she sank on her maiden voyage; the ship could symbolise not only the doomed hopes of the Birlings, but also the misplaced optimism of the pre-war age, destined to end in destruction.

Gerald: 'We've no proof it was the same photograph and therefore no proof it was the same girl' (p. 67)

3

- At first, the Inspector's photographic evidence is persuasive, but the reality, Gerald suggests, could be very different. This vital source of 'proof' is questioned, and Mr and Mrs Birling gratefully accept Gerald's argument.

Morality

4 Eric: 'But don't forget I'm ashamed of you as well – yes both of you.' (p. 57)

- By the end of the play only Eric and Sheila seem to have a clear idea about what is right and what is wrong. This ability to learn a vital moral lesson marks them out from their parents, and the younger generation from the older generation. Eric's statement is a powerful, personal condemnation of his parents.

The relationship between the sexes

5 Mrs Birling: 'When you're married you'll realise that men with important work to do sometimes have to spend nearly all their time and energy on their business. You'll have to get used to that, just as I had.' (p. 3)

- In 1912 middle-class women stayed at home and their husbands went to work. As we shall see, however, there was another reason why Gerald was spending so much of his time during the summer away from Sheila.

6 Sheila: 'I don't dislike you as I did half an hour ago, Gerald. In fact, in some odd way, I rather respect you more than I have ever done' (p. 40)

- Sheila's comments might seem surprising: after all, she has just learned that her fiancé had an affair. Priestley in this way illustrates how she is able to overcome her own self-interest and see the importance of principled action.

Responsibility

7 The Inspector: 'Public men, Mr Birling, have responsibilities as well as privileges.' (p. 41)

- The Inspector succinctly reminds Mr Birling that with those with power and influence also have a sense of duty to others.

8 Eric: 'Whoever that chap was, the fact remains that I did what I did. And mother did what she did. And the rest of you did what you did to her.' (p. 64)

- Like Sheila, Eric learns from the Inspector. He also learns from his own actions, and sees how each member of his family, and Gerald, is responsible for their own behaviour and for the part they played in Eva's death.

Mrs Birling: 'I accept no blame for it at all' (p. 47)

9

- Mrs Birling reveals just how 'cold' and irresponsible she is: despite the Inspector showing her how her actions led directly to Eva's death – and to the death of her unborn baby – Mrs Birling refuses to accept any blame. It makes the final revelation – that the child was her first grandchild – all the more tragic.

Power and class

The Inspector: 'We are members of one body...the time will soon come when, if men will not learn that lesson, then they will be taught it in fire and blood and anguish.' (p. 56)

10

- The Inspector's final speech raises many questions, and the most important are concerned with the future. He seems to be saying that if social change does not happen soon then not only will there be war, but there will also be revolution (of the sort seen in Russia in 1917). Priestley was a socialist and he would argue that, in order to avoid this fate, power has to be redistributed across the classes. In doing so we will create a fairer society.

GRADE **BOOSTER**

```
If you find it difficult to remember a full quotation,
try to remember its main message. For example, in
this quotation, you could just say that the Inspector
warns the Birlings and Gerald about the consequences
of their selfish actions, and write about how, unless
things change, these actions will have huge historical
significance. Making reference to even one key part of
the quotation — such as 'fire and blood and anguish' —
and placing it in a historical context (if appropriate
to the question) can be very effective.
```

Top ten moments in the play

Sheila (*half serious, half playful*): 'Yes – except for all last summer, when you never came near me, and I wondered what had happened to you.' (p. 3)

1

- This is the first clue that all is not what it seems between Sheila and Gerald, despite the excitement of the engagement celebration. The real reason for Gerald's absence will become clearer later.

2

Edna: 'Please, sir, an inspector's called.' (p. 10)

- It is helpful to look very carefully at exactly when this announcement is made. Birling has been holding forth with his views on the importance of looking after oneself. This announcement is therefore very timely as it interrupts the self-satisfied mood.

3

Birling: 'The girl had been causing trouble in the works. I was quite justified.' (p. 17)

- Priestley makes it clear that Birling accepts no responsibility for Eva's death.

4

Sheila: 'So I'm really responsible?' (p. 23)

- In contrast to her father, Sheila accepts responsibility. Priestley is beginning to show us the difference between the younger and older members of the Birling family.

5

Sheila (*laughs rather hysterically*): 'Why – you fool – he knows. Of course he knows. And I hate to think how much he knows that we don't know yet. You'll see. You'll see.' (p. 26)

- This is a very important dramatic moment at the end of Act 1 – a cliffhanger which is designed to 'hook' the audience, who are left wondering about Gerald's involvement and also with a sense that Goole is no ordinary inspector.

6

Mrs Birling: 'As if a girl of that sort would ever refuse money' (p. 47)

- Mrs Birling not only exposes her own ignorance about Eva, but also raises, once again, the prejudices held by many in the middle and upper classes about those they feel are, socially, below them. Eva, of course, does refuse money. Her behaviour throughout is in sharp contrast with that of her social 'superiors'.

7

Mrs Birling: 'He should be made an example of. If the girl's death is due to anybody, then it's due to him…He ought to be dealt with very severely.' (p. 48)

- A wonderful moment of dramatic irony. Eva's death is not down to one person, and Mrs Birling's reductive view of who is responsible will soon backfire on her when she realises that it is Eric, her own son, she is speaking about.

The Inspector: 'One Eva Smith has gone – but there are millions and millions and millions and millions of Eva Smiths and John Smiths still left with us, with their lives, their hopes and fears, their suffering chance of happiness, all intertwined with our lives.' (p. 56)

8

- This is a key message of the play. Eva's name, being close to Eve (in biblical terms the first woman, and symbolic of all women), coupled with the most common surname in Great Britain, clearly gives her universality. She could be anyone, and the Inspector warns us that unless we notice them, and accept how linked we are, then we risk creating conditions that allow people like the Birlings to thrive and the Eva Smiths to die.

Eric (*shouting*): 'And I say the girl's dead and we all helped to kill her – and that's what matters.' (p. 65)

9

- In this climactic moment, Priestley presents Eric and Sheila as frustrated, angry and in direct opposition to their parents and Gerald.

Mr Birling: 'That was the police. A girl has just died – on her way to the infirmary – after swallowing some disinfectant. And a police officer is on his way here -– to ask some – questions–' (p. 72)

10

- These are the last words in the play before the curtain falls. Birling's 'panic-stricken face' and his stuttering speech emphasise that they now understand the enormity of what has just happened and the chance that they have missed.

Wider reading

Non-fiction

- Cook, Judith (1998) *J.B. Priestley*. Bloomsbury.
- Baxendale, John (2014) *Priestley's England: J.B. Priestley and English Culture*. Manchester University Press.

Useful websites

- aninspectorcalls.com – this website is the official website for Stephen Daldry's award-winning stage adaptation of Priestley's play. Aimed at students and teachers, and with a focus very much on this production and on the play as a drama, the website contains many useful resources. The free Teacher's Resource Pack is worth downloading.
- jbpriestley.co.uk – this is the official J.B. Priestley website. It gives lots of information about Priestley's life and times, a lengthy bibliography, and further links. It also includes news on various productions and publications of Priestley's work.

Screen adaptations

- The 2015 BBC production, starring David Thewlis as the Inspector and Miranda Richardson as Mrs Birling, is available on DVD. It received very good reviews and attracted a large audience. It doesn't remain completely faithful to Priestley's script, but is worth watching.
- The 1982 BBC production, starring Nigel Davenport as Mr Birling, is available on YouTube: https://youtu.be/Vukp3EFVweQ The picture quality is not always perfect, but it is worth watching for some very good acting and is perhaps the most faithful production of the play available to watch on screen.

Reviews

Below is a selection of reviews of recent productions of *An Inspector Calls*:

- Sam Wollaston reviews the recent BBC production in the *Guardian*, claiming that it remains relevant today: www.theguardian.com/tv-and-radio/2015/sep/14/an-inspector-calls-this-is-england-90-david-thewlis
- James Delingpole offers a very different view of Priestley's classic play, focusing on the BBC production: www.spectator.co.uk/2015/09/an-inspector-calls-is-poisonous-revisionist-propaganda-which-is-why-the-luvvies-love-it/

Answers

Answers to the 'Review your learning' sections.

Context (p. 18)

1 Context can apply to the political, social and historical background to a text, as well as to biographical influences. It can also refer to literary context.

2 J.B. Priestley was born in Bradford, in Yorkshire.

3 Priestley had a traumatic war: he saw many of his friends die and he was seriously injured.

4 During World War II Priestley was a radio broadcaster for the BBC.

5 *An Inspector Calls* is set in 1912; this date is significant because it is two years before the outbreak of World War I.

6 The play was first performed in Moscow in 1945.

7 The Suffragettes were women who campaigned for equal rights for men and women and for the right to vote.

8 Unity of time, place and action.

9 Socialists seek to have some of the means of production (such as major industries) in the hands of the state; they believe that it is the state's responsibility to look after those who are weak, vulnerable or at the bottom of the social hierarchy. Capitalists believe that private companies are best positioned to look after the interests of society.

10 The *Titanic* could symbolise many things. For instance, it could represent the Birlings' hopes for the evening: filled with hope to begin with, but disastrously sunk by an implacable force. Or it could symbolise the hopes of the country: for many it represented this country's maritime power, but its sinking shook the country's confidence in itself to the core.

Plot and structure (p. 28)

1 *An Inspector Calls* consists of three acts.

2 The play is set in the fictional town of Brumley, which Priestley describes as 'an industrial city in the North Midlands'.

3 The Birlings are celebrating the engagement of their daughter, Sheila, to Gerald Croft, the son of aristocrats Lord and Lady Croft.

4 Mr Birling admits he sacked Eva for leading a group of girls demanding a pay rise. When he refused the pay rise they went out on strike for two weeks; he sacked Eva on their return to work.

5 The Inspector insists that 'it's the way [he likes] to go to work. One person and one line of inquiry at a time. Otherwise there's a muddle.'

6   Sheila breaks off the engagement when she learns that Gerald had an affair with Eva Smith.

7   Gerald met Eva in the Palace Bar.

8   Eva adopts the name 'Mrs Birling' when she asks for help from the Brumley Women's Charity Organisation.

9   Eric accuses his mother of killing Eva Smith by refusing her help.

10 After she has died Eva's body is taken to the infirmary.

Characterisation (p.39)

1   Mr Birling is described as a 'prosperous manufacturer'. His personal characteristics are less promising, however: he is 'portentous' and 'rather provincial' in his speech.

2   Mr Birling describes himself as 'a hard-headed practical business man'.

3   Priestley makes extensive use of dramatic irony: characters say things that unknowingly reveal a lot about themselves. The audience might realise this immediately (as from Mr Birling's references to the *Titanic*) or later on (for example, when we realise why Gerald was rather distant from Sheila in the summer).

4   Mrs Birling is initially described as 'about fifty' and 'a rather cold woman'. Tellingly, in a play where class is so important, she is 'her husband's social superior'.

5   Mrs Birling has many possible 'crimes': she is social snob, treating those below her (including her husband) as inferior; she also treats Eric and Sheila as children; then there is the fact that she turned down a pregnant Eva Smith away from her charity when she was most in need of help. But perhaps her worst offence is her hypocrisy: although she insists that whoever got Eva pregnant should be shown no mercy, she is unable to accept this when she discovers the truth. She is only interested in her reputation.

6   Sheila is described as 'a pretty girl in her twenties, very pleased with life and rather excited.' It is a revealing description because it focuses on the importance she places on appearance, and the Birlings' complacency about life.

7   Both Eric and Sheila learn from their mistakes, and they also accept responsibility for their actions.

8   Eva changes her name to Daisy Renton before meeting Gerald. He did not know her as Eva Smith.

9   The Inspector's surname is Goole, which is a homonym of 'ghoul'. Priestley was interested in the supernatural, and this name has clear connotations with ghosts and the other-world. It certainly adds to the Inspector's air of mystery.

10 Both Eva and Edna are working-class women who have been employed by the Birlings and both apparently lack any real power.

Themes (p.50)

1   A theme is an idea used by a writer in various aspects of the plot; themes are the big ideas that are the intellectual building blocks of the text.

2   Stage directions are instructions given by an author to the director and cast about how best to stage a production. You can see Priestley's in this play as they are all in italics.

3   The lighting is 'pink and intimate until the Inspector arrives', but quite soon changes into something 'harder', similar to a light of interrogation.

4   The *Titanic* could symbolise the conflict between appearance and reality because although it appeared to be 'unsinkable' the reality is, of course, that it did sink on its maiden voyage.

5   The Inspector blames all of the Birlings and Gerald: each of them 'helped to kill her'.

6   The Birlings and Gerald do not do anything that is actually against the law; it could be argued that Eric commits a crime in stealing money from his father.

7   The Suffragettes.

8   The relationship that undergoes the biggest change is probably that between Sheila and Gerald: they begin the play apparently very much in love and celebrating their engagement. The engagement is broken off by Sheila when she learns of Gerald's affair and because she feels they are no longer the same people.

9   The only two characters in the play who accept responsibility and who learn from their experiences are Sheila and Eric; it is they, the 'famous younger generation', who show, through their growing understanding of how we are all linked, that there is hope.

10 Eva does not agree to marry Eric because she feels he does not love her.

Language, style and analysis (p. 59)

1   Domestic drama is concerned with everyday experiences of middle- or working-class characters; such dramas are usually staged in everyday settings, such as a family home.

2   Dialogue is the direct speech of characters involved in conversation.

3   Received Pronunciation is the accent of middle- and upper-middle class England: it not only has strong associations with power but, from a director's pragmatic point of view, is clear and easily understood.

4   Priestley has the Inspector use graphic language to drive home his message.

5   Sheila's language changes to show that she changes and matures.

6 Stagecraft is a term that refers to the staging of a play: how it works on stage, including stage directions, the props used, the lighting, the costumes, and the set and dialogue.

7 Dramatic irony is when the audience are aware of something that a character or characters on stage are not aware of.

8 He uses words such as 'my boy' or 'you youngsters'.

9 Oratory is the art of formal speaking.

10 'Pregnant'.

Tackling the exams (p. 71)

1 Yes, AO4 (the Assessment Objective that specifically addresses spelling, punctuation and grammar) will be assessed for *An Inspector Calls*, unless you are following the OCR specification.

2 No, you cannot take a copy of *An Inspector Calls* into the examination room: it is a 'closed book' examination.

3 It is always a good idea to plan your answer: it helps you organise your thoughts, and should ensure that you are better prepared to answer the question.

4 Use your time wisely: keep an eye on the clock, and try to save a few minutes at the end to go back over your answer to check such things as spelling, punctuation and grammar.

5 Keep your quotations short, embedded and relevant to the point you are making in answering the question.

Assessment Objectives and skills (p. 77)

1 AO1 assesses your ability to maintain a critical style and develop an informed personal response, and it also assesses your use of textual references (including quotations).

2 For AO2 you should be able to analyse the writer's use of language, as well as the form and structure of the play. Evaluation of the writer's meaning, using appropriate literary terms, is also assessed in this AO.

3 AO3 assesses your knowledge and understanding of the contexts the play was written in (this AO is not assessed for *An Inspector Calls* if you are entered for the Eduqas examination).

4 AQA, Eduqas and Edexcel assess AO4 on *An Inspector Calls*. OCR does not.

5 Only you can answer this question, but make sure you know which is your exam board and be clear about which AOs are applicable. It can make a crucial difference to how you answer a question.